Be Your Own Mentor

Other Books in the Briefcase Series

Be Your
Own Mentor

Anne Bruce

New York Chicago San Francisco Lisbon London
Madrid Mexico City Milan New Delhi San Juan
Seoul Singapore Sydney Toronto

The *McGraw·Hill* Companies

1 2 3 4 5 6 7 8 9 0 FGR/FGR 0 9 8 7

ISBN: 978-0-07-148777-1
MHID: 0-07-148777-8

Library of Congress Cataloging-in-Publication Data

Bruce, Anne, 1952–
  Be your own mentor / by Anne Bruce.
    p. cm.
  ISBN 0-07-148777-8 (alk. paper)
  1. Career development.   2. Self-evaluation.   3. Mentoring in business.
I. Title.
  HF5381.B678 2008
  650.1—dc22   2007044369

This publication is designed to provide accurate and authoritative information in regard to the subject matter covered. It is sold with the understanding that neither the author nor the publisher is engaged in rendering legal, accounting, or other professional service. If legal advice or other expert assistance is required, the services of a competent professional person should be sought.
> —From a Declaration of Principles jointly adopted by a Committee
> of the American Bar Association and a Committee of Publishers

McGraw-Hill books are available at special quantity discounts to use as premiums and sales promotions, or for use in corporate training programs. For more information, please write to the Director of Special Sales, McGraw-Hill, 2 Penn Plaza, New York, NY 10128. Or contact your local bookstore.

This book is printed on acid-free paper.

Contents

Preface

Take a moment to look at the front of this book. Look specifically at the title: *Be Your Own Mentor.* Why did you purchase a book with this title? My guess is that you and I interpret *Be Your Own Mentor* to mean the same thing. In order to mentor yourself to a higher level of potential and competency, you must take what I like to call the *whole-person approach* to life.

Our lives at work are not separate from our personal lives. We are one. Henry Ford would often say, "How come when I ask for a pair of hands, I get a human being as well?" The answer is this: one dimension of a person's life is affected by all others. No longer can organizations or their leaders afford to compartmentalize their lives or the lives of their employees. To draw an invisible line that suggests any person can leave his or her personal life at the door when showing up for work totally disregards and ignores the most critical aspects of humanness and self-mentoring.

So let's just say that this invisible line from yesterday's management rulebook is extremely outdated. Workplace psychology teaches us that it is practically impossible for a person to close off his or her personal life on the job, simply because this contradicts human nature at its core. When we take a whole-person approach to our lives and careers many benefits begin to surface, such as sharper innovation and creativity, clearer competencies regarding how we do what we do, brighter intellectual capital, confidence, compassion, and integrity—and that's just for starters. I hope that this whole-person approach is something that gets you excited! This book is going to provide you with a special magnifying glass and the life compasses you need to help these behaviors and talents all come into focus—sharp and specific—directional, not flailing and lost.

Throughout this book, I'll guide you further and more specifically into the process of taking the whole-person approach to self-mentoring. But trust me: it all connects to being your own amazing mentor in your quest for greater career and personal success, at whatever level and competency you are comfortable tackling.

Are You Ready for an Extreme Life-Coaching Makeover?

Here's the deal, right up front. There is no such thing as abra-cadabra when it comes to becoming your own mentor or life coach. With the exception of the mythical pixie dust that exists only at Disneyland and Disney World, there is no fairy dust to sprinkle on, or around, people in hopes of making them happier, healthier, more intuitive, career savvy, money savvy, smarter managers, more loyal, better moms or dads, more loving hus-bands or wives, devoted children, or better in any other way. Achieving those things takes all of *your* hard work and dedica-tion. So to this end I hold you accountable.

You see, this book is also about accountability, not just self-mentoring. Accountability is a critical component of self-mentoring. In my workshops and seminars I often say, "The real learning begins when the class has ended," to drive home the point that I am not the one responsible for the attendees' learning. I can help to facilitate their expertise and ideas and knowledge. It is the learners who are ultimately responsible for following up on the materials and assignments, using my sug-gestions, and applying all they've gathered in class to be the best they can be on the job and at home. I cannot do this for them. The same applies to this book. It is my hope that having this book to help you along the way will make that work less difficult. You are the only one, however, who can sharpen your skills and talents to become your own effective mentor and life coach after you have finished this book.

By asking the question, "Are you ready for an extreme life-coaching makeover?" I am trying to prepare you to get ready to take the lead, roll up your sleeves, and embrace new ideas and unconventional approaches to learning a new way to mentor yourself and be your best life coach in the process. It's time to get on the path of a life-coaching makeover, and this book will give you lots of practical tools to get you started. You don't have to pay anyone anything, hire a career counselor, or go to a therapist to build your confidence to try harder. It's all right here, right now, in this book.

What's Your Makeover Going to Take? And What's It Really Mean to Be Your Own Mentor?

You may be thinking, "Well, what's this life-coaching makeover going to take?" That depends on you. How much of your life do you want to make over? What are you willing to do to take control and learn to be your own mentor in the process? Self-mentoring is not a gene you inherit from a distant relative. It's a learned skill that you hone over time with practice and commitment.

Let's look at it from a survival perspective. Life is about living and surviving, navigating the rough waters, and relishing a new and remarkable view of the horizon. If you're lost in the woods, a compass quickly becomes a key instrument in your survival. So, if you are feeling lost in your career, or even in your personal life too, or if you want to start a business but don't know if it's worth the risk, well, you need a compass to show you the way, right? And that in turn builds greater self-confidence and self-assurance. Self-mentoring is all about *self*.

Here's where the *self* part comes in. You are the compass. I bet you were thinking that the compass was a totally separate instrument from yourself. It's not. You are the instrument. You are the precious container that holds the answers—the lightning in the bottle—and you are the bottle. You have everything you need to navigate your life and mentor yourself to higher grounds. This book is going to show you how a life-coaching and self-mentoring approach is within reach and easier to implement than you ever dreamed possible, whether your issues and challenges are in the workplace or in your own backyard. Here's how to recognize some of the signs that you may be overdue for a life-coaching and self-mentoring make-over.

You're Ready for a Life-Coaching Makeover if You Are:

- Confused and angry about your present job
- Having a difficult time with personal and business relationships
- Sick and tired of always being sick and tired (physically or mentally)
- Having problems making decisions easily
- Never happy with the outcome of your efforts
- Always feeling like a victim
- Incessantly whining about your life
- Repeating the same old bad habits
- Getting nowhere fast
- Always feeling afraid, but not sure what of
- Feeling like life is happening *at you* instead of *for you*
- Attracting all the wrong people, places, and things, but unable to figure out why
- Wishing you were working at something else, for someone else
- Dreading going home from work, or dreading going to work from home
- Afraid of taking risks of any kind
- Not feeling in charge of your own life

- Looking for a simple-to-use formula that will give you the tools you need to take charge and guide yourself in the direction of a life you so richly deserve and more—short of hiring someone else to do it for you, tell you what you're doing wrong and how to do it right, or move in with you and live in your spare bedroom until you get it right.

A Go-to and Keep-It-Going Resource

Let this book be your official "go-to" and "keep-it-going" resource. I promise it will not tell you how to hire a career counselor or find a life coach. You already know how to do that. And do not misinterpret my perception of these services; I think they are great and they can often be a good and solid first step. I do lots of life coaching and mentoring for people from all over the world, and I even promote using a life coach heavily on my radio shows. Getting a formal coach can be a great way to kick-start your business, relationships, and overall direction of well-being. What I don't recommend in my seminars, or write about in my books, is becoming perpetually dependent on others when it comes to self-development and professional development. It's easy to fall into the "tell me what to do and how to do it" trap.

I have met folks at my seminars who confide to me during a break that they have been in therapy or using a life coach for 10 years, and some even longer. However, after a reasonable amount of time, I believe most of us want to learn to do things ourselves, figure things out, and solve our own work and life problems. If it takes 10 years of therapy and professional coaching to get the answers, then I'm guessing that person may not be truly motivated to take accountability for his or her own life, learn new lessons, and become a self-directed learner. Or, frankly, this question always comes to mind: "What is this person afraid of?" I wrote this book so that you will figure "it" out sooner rather than later and become accountable and self-reliant in the process, less fearful of the unknown, and more confident in yourself. The key is to count on yourself first and foremost. Why is this important? Because the only one you can ultimately count on in the end is you.

There are two constants that support the important concept of self-mentoring at any level of personal and professional development and growth:

1. Understanding that you will one day leave this life
2. Accepting that you, and you alone, are the only one in charge of this life until that time comes

So now that you—and no one else—are the one in charge, how will you go forward with gusto? What will you do to make your career stronger, your relationships more meaningful, or your plans for the future more exciting? How will you be accountable, and what do you plan to do about it?

That's the real question and the real response to anyone who claims to be truly accountable. What do you plan to do with your newfound accountability?

I, for one, believe you'll be better equipped to answer that after you uncover the powerful, four-part, self-mentoring formula within this book. As I said earlier, this book will become your keep-it-going resource as you go through each step of the process.

A Do-It-Yourself Guide to Achieving Greater Career and Personal Success

This book was written to guide you in your quest for achieving greater career and personal success. It provides guidelines and assessments, tools and practices for maintaining high levels of life performance and productivity, a safe and happy work and home environment, and hope for a better tomorrow. That's the purpose of this book. That's the challenge, and, ultimately, that is the expedition you are preparing to embark on.

Whether you are a manager, supervisor, entrepreneur, aspiring entrepreneur, part-time student, part-time worker, retiree, or a combination of several of these roles, you most likely are not willing to spend tons of time looking for the answers to every challenge in your life. Surveys frequently show that as time goes on more people have less time to find what they are looking for or willingness to spend that time investigating what's most important to them. Life happens and people usually have other demands to deal with, such as workplace issues, children, aging parents, money problems, health issues, and more.

We live in a breakneck-speed world, where *fast and practical* is the mantra and where ready references for managers and life-coaching tools, like the ones offered in the Briefcase Book Series, are desperately needed. *Be Your Own Mentor* is a book whose time has come—a time for practical self-guidance, complete with worksheets, real-life coaching tools, assessments, and the inspiration to fuel and guide you, the reader, in making the most of yourself at whatever level is fitting and appropriate for you at this place and time in your life.

Businesspeople today want a fast and easy way to get on track and stay on track. When I am teaching my seminars and workshops around the globe, participants appreciate when I can give them a formula that they can use and apply to their individual circumstances and unique personalities. Why? Because a formula that can be easily followed becomes a person's roadmap or blueprint for furthering their success and allows the journey to be navigable, one baby step at a time. When we use formulas to guide a life process, we are able to "chunk things down" into bite-sized portions of understandability and comprehension. We simplify the big picture and lessen the chances of feeling overwhelmed in a world where information and guidelines are being thrown at us from every perspective.

Figure P.1 shows the formula you'll be using in this book.

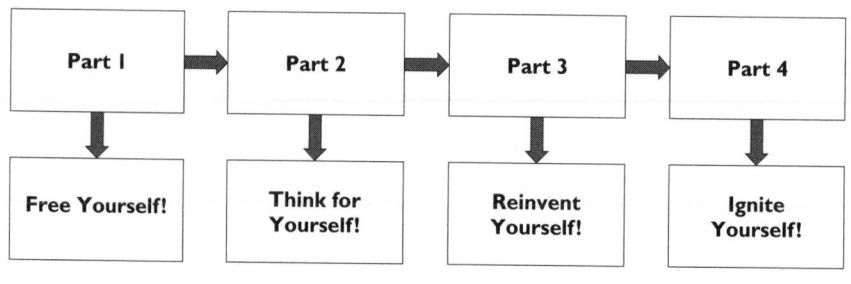

Lightning

in

a

Bottle

=

YOU—behaving as your own mentor—an innovative thinker, decision maker, solution finder, problem solver, and change agent. The lightning is *within* you. You are the bottle—the precious container that holds the talent and possibilities for a better, more productive, and joyful tomorrow. Now, how you get there will be the result of your reading and applying the information in this book and using this critical four-part formula for achieving greater career and personal success.

Figure P.1. Stay Competitive. Be Confident. A 4-Part Do-It-Yourself Life-Coaching Formula for Becoming Your Own Mentor.

Fitness Counts—Are You Up for the Challenge?

Now that you've looked at the four-part formula you'll be using, remember the first words at the top of the formula: Stay competitive. Be confident. These aren't passive requests; they are action terms, and this is where fitness counts.

Think of this book as your personal "life gym" where there are no dues to pay or membership requirements. There is no aerobics class or equipment to jump on and ride. The sweat you'll produce will be "sweat equity," not the kind you perspire while using the treadmill. When it comes to making this book a life tool for greater success, fitness counts. As you can tell, I'm not talking about your weight, eyesight, physical strength, endurance, illnesses you might be living with, cholesterol count, or blood pressure reading. I'm talking about life fitness—your overall well-being when it comes to your fitness as it relates to the following:

- Family relationships
- Marriage
- Children
- Friendships
- Business relationships
- Management skills
- Financial savvy
- Happiness
- Loving your job
- Igniting your passion
- Activating your higher potential
- Firing yourself up and staying motivated
- Spiritual well-being
- Teambuilding
- Igniting your many intelligences and competencies
- Getting organized
- Living up to your greater potential and possibility
- Reaching your goals for work and life

Within the pages of this book you'll find a powerful new way to activate your greater potential and become the primary navigator of your own destiny. But all of this takes muscle if you are to play a significant role in the process. How will you build your self-mentoring muscle? How will you select and utilize the best ideas for you?

Selecting the Best Ideas for You in This Book

Whether you're reading Chapter 2, "Traditional Career Planning Will Be Gone as We Know It," or Chapter 10, "Why Your Self-Esteem Is Directly Related to Your Intelligence," you'll find within this book some of the best and most useful ideas on creating a jubilant and uplifting self-mentoring program—a program that fits your specific needs and requirements. These ideas and suggestions in the program come from a wide variety of experts and sources—businesspeople like you who have been mentoring themselves along the way in a fashion that works for them and then getting the results they've always wanted.

Other ideas in this book come from many talented people— some you have heard of and some you haven't. Many are well-known managers and leaders, others not so well known but noticeably effective in their self-mentoring and management styles. Some are authors, consultants, scholars, and entrepreneurs. Some are living and some are dead. Maybe you have heard of these people and their companies, or perhaps you've read about them and admire their people skills and talent for bringing out the best in others. Regardless of your familiarity with the experts in this book, all of them have proven performance records when it comes to creating extraordinary opportunity for themselves and their organizations and for leaving their indelible imprint on the hearts and minds of those who have been fortunate enough to work with them or know them as friends and family.

So where do the experts and examples in this book come from? They come from all sectors of the global workplace— business, professions, politics, government, social and nonprofit organizations, manufacturing, health care, technology, and more. Their contributions to this book consist of interviews I have conducted in person and by phone. Plus, there are organizations and people in this book whom I have yet to meet in person or interview. Yet, I've studied and researched them and their organizations for years, showcasing their invigorating and mentor-boosting styles in my keynote speeches and workshops I facilitate around the world. When it comes to the subject of being your own mentor, lots of people are doing it right and love to tell their stories. You'll find those stories and real-world examples from which you can glean the gems of how to be your own mentor right here.

The Purpose of This Book

I wrote this book with a specific purpose in mind. That purpose was not just to have this book be read by managers and then put on the shelf to collect dust. I wrote *Be Your Own Mentor* to be *used* by managers and others, including you, as a valuable field guide to help shape and increase your chances of success. I wrote this book with the explicit idea that the four-part formula I have developed over years of research, writing, and training will give you some of the tools you need—specifically, a compass—to find your way to greater prosperity and inner happiness.

My goal while writing this book was that you, the reader, would be able to easily glean important pieces of information and apply them in the most appropriate and effective way on the job and at home, as quickly as possible. The format and style of a book such as this one in the Briefcase Series allows that to happen quite easily.

Manager's Call to Action

In all of the Briefcase Books I have written, I have made a personal request of my readers. Here it is again. My request is that you take the abundant wellspring of information in this book, information that will hopefully inform and inspire you, and interpret it as your own personal call to action as it pertains to

These boxes give you tips and tactics for being smart as a new manager and help you to develop important self-mentoring skills as your own life coach.

These boxes provide warnings for where things could go wrong when you're dealing with employees and mentoring.

Here you'll find how-to hints to make managing and self-mentoring go more easily.

Every subject has its special jargon and terms. These boxes provide definitions of these concepts.

Want to know how others have done it? Look for these boxes.

Here you'll find specific procedures you can follow to understand various management tasks and life-coaching tools.

How can you make sure you won't make a mistake when managing? You can't, but these boxes will give you practical advice on how to minimize the possibility.

becoming your own mentor. In other words, do something with this information!

Remember earlier I asked you to think about if you were ready for an extreme life-coaching makeover and told you that, if so, such action required accountability, and then I asked what you planned to do with that accountability? Doing something—anything—with the gems of advice inside this book will make them come alive and become a reality for you.

Special Features

The idea behind the books in the Briefcase Book Series is to give you practical information written in a friendly, person-to-person style. The chapters are short, deal with tactical issues, and include lots of examples, as I mentioned earlier. They also feature eye-catching icons and boxes, checklists, and side-bars, all designed to give you different types of specific information.

A description of what you'll find to help guide you in this book is located on p. xx.

Let these special features, listed on the left, guide you in your pursuit to learn more about self-mentoring and critical life-coaching methods. When used effectively, these features provide speedy learning and faster reading for busy managers.

Acknowledgments

For anyone who knows me, it is no secret that I am all about family and the inner circle of friends I call my extended family. Without all of you, I would not be able to write this book or all the others I've written in the past dozen years. And so it is here that I thank all of my family and extended family—you know who you are—from the bottom of my heart for their unconditional love and support, belief in me, devotion to helping me succeed, and immeasurable loyalty on every front. At the core of my greatest appreciation is my immense gratitude to my daily cheering gallery—my husband David W. Thomley and my daughter Autumn Kelly Mostovoj. Thank you both for always holding me in the light of your love and for championing my ideas and work for all these many years. I love you beyond anything I could describe in words. You inspire me to be my best and to make you proud. I have learned the life-changing lessons of self-mentoring and the extraordinary power of the human spirit from both of you.

In addition, I am fortunate to have two families—the one that I am related to by blood and friendship and the one I am related to via the publishing world. McGraw-Hill has been my publishing family for a dozen years. I'd like to thank one of my publishing mentors and life-coaches while writing this book, Senior Editor Jeanne Glasser. Thanks, Jeanne, for your graciousness, advice, and friendship through the years. Your mindful guidance has been the net underneath me as I've leaped from one page to the next in this book. Also, a big thank-you goes to my editor on this book, Donya Dickerson. This was my first time working with Donya and it's been an absolute pleasure every step of the way. You're a pro in a tough business, Donya, and your good work shows in this book! What readers can't see in this book are your kindness, consideration, and easy-to-be-friends-with nature.

To the awesome and talented team of editors and production staff at McGraw-Hill Publishing, you are all amazing and truly the unsung heroes of the publishing world. You all make the production effort of creating books appear seamless. It's fun to work with all of you. And to the copyeditors, especially Ellen Lohman, book cover designers, and to my production editor Debbie Masi, you save the day with your valued input and creative flair. Thank you to everyone for working your magic on this book.

A special thank-you goes to Elly Mixsell Shelswell-White, the amazing lady who designs my annebruce.com Web site, all of my workbook materials, seminar handouts, and several graphics featured in this book. Thanks, Elly, for being my friend first, for always making me look good, and for taking pride in my work as if it were your own. Your originality, creative energy, and devotion to each and every project we've worked on together for the past 12 years is greatly appreciated!

And finally, a great, big THANK-YOU to every person out there who has at one time or another attended one of my seminars, workshops, or keynote speeches, and to all of you who keep coming back, bringing friends and colleagues, and buying books—you're simply the best! Your heartfelt stories, e-mails, letters, and helpful feedback continue to enrich my life by allowing me to be a part of yours.

Before concluding these acknowledgments, I'd like to dedicate this book to my dear friend and life coach and mentor Joan Smith. Your time in my life was much too brief. I cherish your words of love and continue to implement your sage advice and wisdom each and every day. And to your husband Wilson, thank you, Dear Friend, for continuing to lend to me your inspiration, love, and support. You and "Jazz" never miss a beat.

About the Author

Anne Bruce is a bestselling author and inspirational speaker and trainer on the topics of human behavior, professional development, and personal growth. She's facilitated workshops on *How to Be Your Own Mentor*, the topic upon which this book is based, from Las Vegas to Washington, DC, Geneva to London, Dubai to Delhi, and at business conferences and international meetings and management forums around the globe.

Anne is the author of the bestselling communications business book *Perfect Phrases for Documenting Employee Performance Problems* (McGraw-Hill), *Discover True North: A 4-Week Program to Ignite Your Passion and Activate Your Potential* (McGraw-Hill), *How to Motivate Every Employee* (part of the McGraw-Hill Mighty Manager Series), *Motivating Employees* and *Building A High Morale Workplace* (part of the Briefcase

Book Series), *Leaders—Start to Finish: A Road Map for Training and Developing Leaders at All Levels* (ASTD Press), and the popular bestseller *Speaker! Build a Profitable Speaking and Training Business—An Insider's Guide* (ASTD Press).

Anne has appeared on the *CBS Evening News with Dan Rather* and on the *Charlie Rose Show*. She's worked extensively in broadcast journalism and has been interviewed by distinguished print media such as *Newsweek* magazine, *USA Today*, the *Times* (London), and the *Wall Street Journal*. She's been both a guest author and featured speaker for the White House, the CIA, FBI, the Pentagon, JetBlue, Southwest Airlines, the Conference Board of Europe, Coca-Cola, Sprint, Blue Cross and Blue Shield, Ben & Jerry's, GEICO, Barnes & Noble Booksellers, Sprint, and Baylor University Medical Center. She's instructed programs at both Harvard and Stanford Law Schools and hosts her own radio talk show called *Anne Bruce Life Coach* in several major media markets. Anne also offers one-on-one life coaching to "kick-start" people on their way to becoming their own mentor.

For more information on workshops and keynote presentations or life-coaching sessions associated with this book and others by Anne, visit her Web site at www.annebruce.com to get a workshop outline and details on how you can bring this program or one-on-one coaching into your organization. You also can e-mail her at anne@annebruce.com or call 214-507-8242 for more information.

Anne and her husband David live in Charleston, South Carolina, and enjoy the beach life with their two 100-pound dogs Tex and Heidi. Anne continues to be recognized for her highly entertaining and award-winning platform speeches to multinational companies worldwide.

Introduction

Dump the "Gotta Get Me a Coach" Approach and Start Looking Within!

There's a popular attitude going around in the workplace, and it goes something like this: "Gotta get me a coach!"

No matter how great a life coach is, he or she can do nothing for you if you don't have the gumption, motivation, or accountability to create your own destiny. You've got to be willing to look within for all of those things. A life coach only helps to facilitate your future success and progress; only you can make it a reality. That brings me to the next point. If you have all of those things—gumption, motivation, desire—then what's stopping you from getting on with becoming your own life coach or mentor?

> **Life Coach** A person who advises and lends support and guidance on a wide variety of life challenges, such as career planning, money matters, personal relationships, setting goals, sharpening skill sets, making major life changes, and sorting through critical decisions. Life-coaching fees are wide and varied. Some coaches charge monthly retainers of between $300 and $3,000 and up, and others charge by the hour, from $75 an hour to more than $250 an hour. Life coaches are not considered the same as executive coaches.

Setting the Stage for Your Progress and Growth

This part of the book, in my opinion, is critical, because it sets the stage for you to experience a major paradigm shift. This

> ### Here's How It May Sound
>
> Boy oh boy, I'm miserable in this job, and look at me, I never get promoted, and I'm not crazy about my personal life much either, and I'm overweight and I can't get motivated to go to the gym, and I've not paid my bills on time in months, and I probably won't meet the deadline my boss gave me for Tuesday's staff meeting, and . . . well . . . the answer is pretty clear. All I gotta do is get me a life coach and that will fix everything! He or she will tell me exactly what to do and how to do it. My coach will get me back on track and help me to live a better life and reach my higher potential. All I gotta do is get a coach and life will be good! Yeah, that's the ticket!

major paradigm shift is a mind shift that goes from the "I gotta get me a life coach who can tell me what to do" mentality to adopting a stronger, more courageous, self-reliant attitude that says, "Hey, I *can* do this myself. I can be my own mentor and take the initiative if I have the right tools and a plan of action to make it happen." Well, guess what? You're holding the tools and the plan of action in your hands now. They are in this book.

This is a call to action for you to dump the "Gotta get me a coach" approach to life. If that's been your approach up to now, then here's where you leave it behind. As I've said before, I'm not against professional life coaching as a kick start to helping someone get moving in the right direction of his or her life or career path. I conduct coaching sessions by phone almost every week, and I've had the good fortune to work with and present coaching programs on the public-speaking circuit with some of the top life coaches and executive coaches in America. But a coach is not, and should not be, a long-term answer to fix a broken life. Only you can look within and find the long-term answer for repairing and redirecting your life. Your self-transformation can be accomplished only by you and no one else.

Your Self-Transformation Starts Here

Coaches are people just like you, and you may not know this, but in many cases you can do exactly the same thing a coach does for you and not spend a nickel. Or you can spend very little to get going and then take it from there. Now, are there exceptions to this? Of course, and you may be one of them, and therefore hiring someone to assist you for an indefinite amount of time might be just what the doctor ordered.

There's no doubt that there is a coaching explosion, especially in executive coaching, in this country. And the one thing a great coach can do that you cannot is look you in the eye and tell you the things you may not want to hear or may be in denial about—things such as, "You need to listen more carefully, because you're missing the point in almost every meeting with your staff" or "Face up to the fact that you tend to bully your people and then you kiss up to the board members you feel can benefit you most."

Coaches who tell it like it is can be highly effective, especially when it comes to delivering hard-to-take, unpleasant messages about our behaviors. When we truthfully confront and deal with our behaviors and faux pas, we are in a much stronger position to lead others and take on new challenges in management and in our personal lives with greater confidence.

> **Key Term**
>
> **Executive Coach** Executive coaches typically work with higher-level managers and leaders. Their clients may already be high-ranking executives who want to sharpen their skills and take their talents to another company or to the next level in an organization. Their clients also may be aspiring executives and on the fast track to the executive office in their organization. In many cases, the organization itself will pay for and provide the executive coach. Executive coaching fees can range from $100 an hour to $750 or even $1,200 an hour, depending on the level at which the executive coaches are coaching their clients and the cities in which they work.

Your ability to get things moving in your life with the valued feedback you receive from a coach and then take over and keep things going yourself comes down to your preparedness and your willingness to hear, receive, and do something with the information you are provided. Once you have the knowledge, you hold the power.

It's important to fully grasp and understand the overall bigger picture of how enormously powerful you can be on your own when it comes to navigating your personal and professional success. Am I motivating you? I hope so. I know that with the right tools and guidance you can be the primary navigator of your life and learn to rely on yourself for the right answers. It's a self-transformational process, and you are the architect in charge of how the process takes shape and how your life structure is built, step-by-step.

The first step in your self-transformation is to shift your paradigm.

Take Control—Become the Primary Navigator in Your Life

Any self-transformation starts with a shift in our thinking and how we subsequently see ourselves. We fear shifting our paradigms, or beliefs and ideas we've held onto for so long, because that shift represents that we must somehow change or that we may have been wrong to begin with. And to many people, psychologically, any sort of change equals loss, and loss could entail losing hope and perhaps even losing the feeling of possibility. Well, I am here to tell you that this simply does not have to be the case. In order to go through any significant self-transformation, change is required, which can be, and usually is, a valuable experience of growth and learning. Even bad situations in life oftentimes bring about positive change in the end. From the seeds of adversity spring prosperity. Therefore, shifting our paradigms is required in order to best transform our lives and our vision

> **CAUTION!**
>
> ### Avoid the Downshift
>
> Take caution. The problem often lies in the act of actually shifting. People tend to shift downward. They don't give themselves credit for what they can be or what they are capable of becoming or doing in this lifetime. They shift downward. They settle for less and compromise. Remember what Eleanor Roosevelt once said: "If you're going to compromise, compromise up!" So the answer is to start shifting upward! When we shift upward we shift our paradigms into a higher gear of greater potential and hope for a better tomorrow. To use a driving analogy, you can actually feel yourself rising to a higher level of consciousness while merging onto life's higher road.

of the future. But sometimes it's harder than it seems.

> **Key Term**
>
> **Paradigm**   A way of thinking that serves as a pattern or model for something, especially one that forms the basis of a theory, belief, or methodology.

Start with Four Self-Transformational Questions

Self-mentoring starts with a series of four blocks of paradigm-shifting questions. By shifting, I mean changing your perspectives or views on things in a way that moves you upward. We activate this positive movement by asking ourselves specific questions. These questions actually begin the self-transformation process, and it's something you can do all on your own. Take a look at Figure 1.1 and see how you can shift your paradigm thinking upward by examining these initial questions and know that by simply answering a few basic questions to get started you can begin your own major self-transformation. This is the first step in becoming your own mentor.

Take time to really study and answer these questions in the illustration. Most folks say they want to change their lives, and so they jump into something too quickly, like enrolling in grad school when they are already feeling overwhelmed at home and

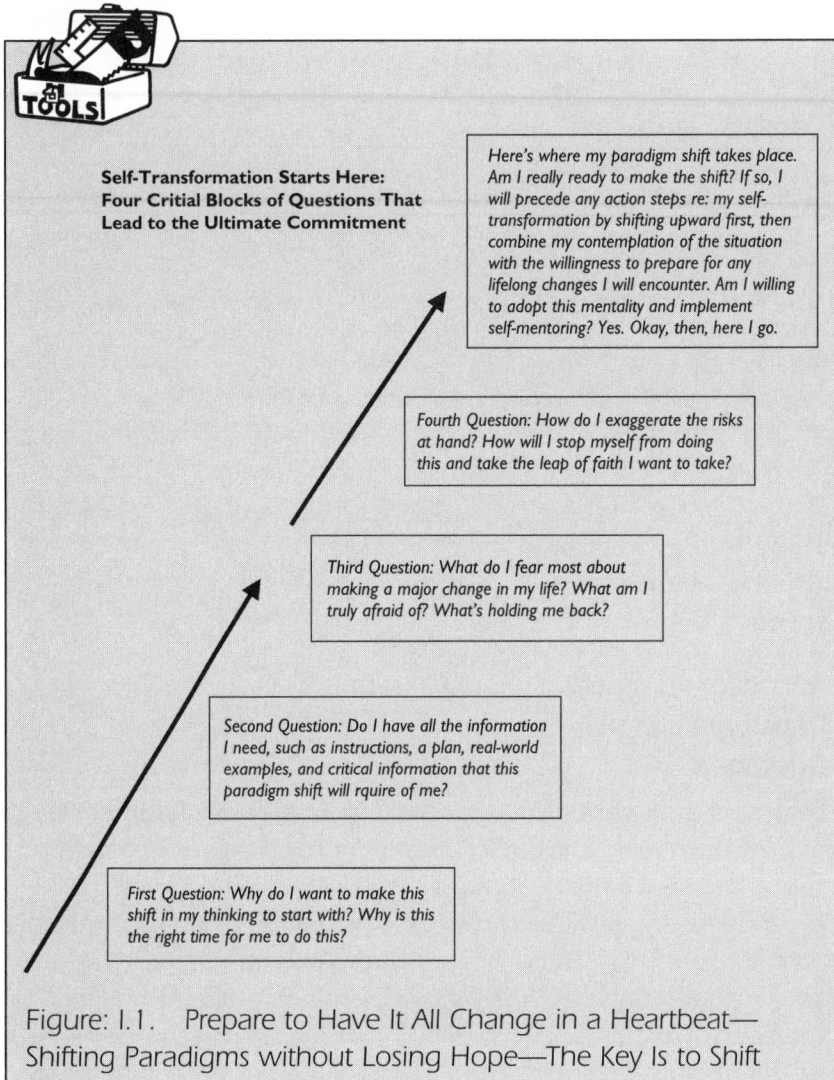

Self-Transformation Starts Here:
Four Critial Blocks of Questions That
Lead to the Ultimate Commitment

Here's where my paradigm shift takes place. Am I really ready to make the shift? If so, I will precede any action steps re: my self-transformation by shifting upward first, then combine my contemplation of the situation with the willingness to prepare for any lifelong changes I will encounter. Am I willing to adopt this mentality and implement self-mentoring? Yes. Okay, then, here I go.

Fourth Question: How do I exaggerate the risks at hand? How will I stop myself from doing this and take the leap of faith I want to take?

Third Question: What do I fear most about making a major change in my life? What am I truly afraid of? What's holding me back?

Second Question: Do I have all the information I need, such as instructions, a plan, real-world examples, and critical information that this paradigm shift will rquire of me?

First Question: Why do I want to make this shift in my thinking to start with? Why is this the right time for me to do this?

Figure: I.1.   Prepare to Have It All Change in a Heartbeat—Shifting Paradigms without Losing Hope—The Key Is to Shift Upward!

on the job, or marrying someone too fast, or changing jobs too quickly, letting someone go in the department who could have been saved, or some other action that might spell regret—only to find out that they didn't take the time to ask a few basic questions that would quickly lift the fog and help them to shift their paradigms in a way that could have long-lasting effectiveness. So the first step is to shift upward by responding to four blocks of questions. The second step is to take control of your life.

Take Control—You Are the Sole Navigator in Your Life

When you become your own mentor, you become the author of your life story.

The day you come into this world, an amazing gift is bestowed upon you: the gift of becoming the sole navigator and author of your life story. You are continuously writing your story both at home and on the job. If you don't like the story so far, fine. Rewrite it. When you see yourself as the sole author and navigator of your life, you begin making a conscious decision to fully accept ownership of personal and professional accountability for where you will go and how you will get there. That's what being your own mentor is all about.

Remember this: no matter where you are in your life at this time, or how desperate you may be feeling about your job or your future, you have everything you need within you to change your course and to achieve greater happiness and career success. Earlier in this book I told you that you are the precious container that holds the lightning in the bottle and that within you lies a powerful internal compass that will guide you toward greater confidence and courage when you need it most.

Believing that this exists within you is not an option. It is a requirement. Only when you believe this can you mentor yourself toward the courage and hope necessary to get where you want to go in this life.

Mentor Yourself toward Courage and Hope

It takes guts to be your own mentor. Why? Because it requires courage to make significant changes in our lives, especially when those changes require us to make new and brave decisions. It requires even more guts to take charge and be your own mentor. By taking charge yourself, you have no one to blame or hold accountable but you.

There is a song from the play *The King and I* which begins, "Make believe you're brave and the trick will take you far. You may be as brave as you make believe you are." Have you ever had to make believe you were brave? Maybe you had to put up a good front on the job when you feared layoffs, or maybe you had to evacuate your department after a bomb scare, or maybe you had to act brave for your kids and husband when you feared the results of a mammogram or other health-related tests.

When we do any of these things, we are mentoring ourselves toward courage. It's the kind of courage that comes from within and gives us the strength to keep moving forward and learn from the situation at hand. If you're going to be your own mentor, then you have to first learn to mentor yourself toward courage and away from fear. You've got to build your courage muscle.

Build Your Courage Muscle

I mention earlier in this book that I've had the honor of sharing the public speaking platform with some amazing life and career coaches. One in particular I happen to admire greatly is Barbara Poole, a famous master-certified executive career coach with Success Builders, Inc., of Charleston, South Carolina. I admire Barbara because she exemplifies the kind of coach I would hire. She walks the talk, every step of the way.

In a recent interview with Barbara about this book and over a green-tea Frappucino, at a "third-space" office setting, located in a Charleston-area Barnes and Noble bookstore, this highly respected success coach gave me some pointers on what it takes to build your courage muscle, especially before making a career change. She, herself, has morphed her career through the years. Barbara's boundaryless career has included roles as a psychotherapist, university career center director, HR manager, organizational development consultant, and currently she's added to her resume the job of columnist for the *Charleston Regional Business Journal.*

According to Barbara, the fear that often accompanies making a career change is one of the most powerful emotions we experience and it has the luxury of being self-reinforcing because the comfort zone it keeps us in is a safe, albeit, boring, place to be. "So what if you decided to stare down the fear factor? What would it take to develop your courage muscle when it comes to making the career change you claim you have been waiting for a long time?" asks Barbara.

Here are some of Barbara's tips when it comes to cultivating the courage required to take the plunge:

Step 1: Just begin. Dive in. It's the only way to begin swimming to the other side. Barbara adds that she's encountered many people who too often use self-help books and inventory assessments as a hiding place when they have a sense of what they want, but are afraid to get started.

Step 2: Ask yourself, "What's the best that could happen?" When it comes to planning for a career transition, a lot of energy gets expended on catastrophizing. Barbara recommends turning the "What if?" question upside down, using it to paint a picture of the most fabulous outcome you can imagine. "We're always more likely to achieve what we focus on," says Barbara.

Step 3: Manage your self-talk. The career transition process is fertile ground for the gremlin who sits inside your head and likes to tell you that you're not smart/talented/qualified/creative/lucky enough to get and keep the job you really want. Substitute the negative commentary with a positive proclamation that says

Navigator of Courage and Hope

Smart Managing   For more than 20 years, Dr. Pam Hinds has served as a real-world mentor and navigator of hope and courage for St. Jude Children's Research Hospital in Memphis, Tennessee. As the director of nursing research at St. Jude, Dr. Hinds mentors staff, patients, and patients' families, sustaining hope and courage by focusing on the moment-to-moment miracles of the day.

Here are some of Dr. Hinds's suggestions when it comes to mentoring others toward courage in an environment where fear for what *might be* and hope for what *can be* come together on a daily basis.

- Be a real person to those who need you; get involved with their lives.
- Remember that everything good you do on the job goes beyond the walls of where you work.
- Focus on what is most meaningful to others and meet those human needs as best you can.
- Do not sacrifice human connection for productivity.
- Know that much can be said with few words.
- In the midst of extreme intensity and sadness, look to the many miracles of survival that surround you.
- Appreciate that even dying patients have hope and courage and it is your job to sustain that.
- Have a mission. At St. Jude the mission is "to find cures for children with catastrophic illnesses through research and treatment." When you have a clear mission, you will draw the right people to you and to your organization.
- Honor every relationship.
- Look to the future and share your hope and belief in miracles.

you have what it takes to capture and master the job of your dreams.

Step 4: Get your hands on good information. Get your hands on accurate data about the job, industry, and companies you are interested in and study them backward and forward. Make sure you have a handle on the reality of your circumstances, including your budgetary and financial and personal needs, such as childcare and transportation.

Step 5: Connect with the people who can help you achieve your objectives. Lean into your professional·and support networks and allow your contacts to help you with the transition.

Barbara Poole can be reached at coachbarbara@success buildersinc.com.

Fear—The Great Debilitator

Franklin D. Roosevelt said, "The only thing we have to fear is fear itself." It is difficult to be your own mentor and life coach when you are immersed in fear. In fact, it is practically impossible.

Fear is the great immobilizer of managers, or of anyone, for that matter. However, if you practice being your own mentor, then in the face of what frightens you most, if you choose to take bold actions, you can overcome your fear and anxiety. And yes, you can do this on your own with the right tools and techniques.

It's important to understand that fear will completely immobilize you if you let it. Fear can keep you from being the best manager or supervisor, mom or dad, sister or brother, best friend, or volunteer. In other words, fear will stop you dead in your tracks if you let it.

Fear Is, and Always Will Be, Powerless over You

If you really want to be your own mentor, then you've got to understand one cardinal rule when it comes to dealing with fear, and that is that fear has absolutely no power over you—zip. However, what does have power over you and can debilitate you is how you *feel* about your fears. The fear itself cannot

A Powerful Remedy

There is a cure for fear. It's called courage.

Be Scared to Death and Then Take Action!

David K. Reynolds teaches a program referred to as "Lifeway" and offers training called Constructive Living, using practices from Japanese theories called Morita and Naikan. In the Morita training the mantra is, "Be scared to death and then do what you have to do." The message is that you can recite affirmations and practice techniques to overcome your fears, but without action in the face of what you fear, you'll never really experience the fear itself, the risk required to confront it, and the exhilaration of success afterward.

Today, we often put the drive for success first, then follow that with the need to feel good about ourselves. If you're anxious, take a pill. Tense or nervous? There's a pill for that, too. Depressed? No problem. The principles behind Dr. Reynolds's teachings are truly those of self-mentoring and life coaching. He teaches that it is perfectly okay to feel anxiety or sadness or fear, because feeling these emotions is what drives people to take action and then do something about what's been holding them back.

touch you, but how you feel about it can. Mentoring yourself away from those feelings is how you rise above the fear itself.

Self-mentoring helps us to understand that we can overcome our fears when we implement courage against them. Here's an example.

I have a colleague who is very much afraid to fly. However, she must fly because her job with the training company she works for takes her all over the globe. Of course, she could say, "I'm deathly afraid of flying and so I will just have to miss that important meeting in London next week," but that would not be truthful to her or to others. The fact is, she can fly and still be afraid to fly at the same time.

My friend's ability to face her fear of flying does not require that she be totally comfortable with being on a 757 airliner. But because she is her own coach and mentor, it does require that she do three things each time she flies:

1. She must buy a plane ticket.

Blowing up the Box Minimizes Being Immobilized inside the Box

Being your own mentor requires much more than just stepping outside the box, as the popular managerial saying goes. It sometimes requires blowing up the very box you are confined by. The results may not always be pleasant, but what's your alternative? Quit? No way. When we choose not to face our fears, we choose the possibilities of languishing in regret and wondering what life could have been like if we weren't so frightened.

---

2. She must get herself to the airport and show up for the flight on time.
3. She must board the flight when it's time to depart for her destination.

Being your own mentor requires showing up by putting one foot in front of the other. It also means facing your fears head on, taking calculated risks, and then enjoying the good feeling that comes from not having given in to panic or given away a piece of your resolve and courage to the very thing you are most afraid of.

It's certainly not easy, but it is doable with mental resolve and commitment to achieving a better, stronger you. Are you up for the challenge?

Often the people to whom I speak or for whom I write want easy answers or prescriptions for a fast fix. I've become pretty good at giving advice, but when it comes to the topic of being courageous, I have found

Memorable Quote

"I was brought up to believe that how I saw myself was more important than how others saw me."

—Anwar El-Sadat, former Egyptian President

that everyone has his or her own story to tell. And it is from these unique perspectives that I have learned the most from all of you. I also have learned that everyone's been courageous in his or her life at one time or another. Here's my question to those people: "In what ways have you mustered the courage to take action in your life, overcoming paralyzing fear or dread?" Know what? Everyone has a story to tell when it comes to describing the role courage has played in his or her life. What's yours? Write it down.

Describe a time when you had to expand your capacity as a person and act with great courage. Perhaps you were facing adversity and hardship. What enabled you to get through this particular time in your life? When you open up to answering these questions, you begin to know yourself and better understand why you've made the choices that you have made. Write your responses here:

_____

_____

_____

_____

_____

Maybe you are pleased with these choices and maybe you are not. Either way, you can navigate your life toward different outcomes if you simply make new choices along the way.

Courage Is a Choice

You may not be able to *plan* to act courageously in this life, but you can *choose* to act courageously. Just talking and writing about our own and others' courageous moments is one way we coach ourselves down a path of preparedness and opportunity.

We mentor ourselves when we take on these decisions and actions, and by doing so we demonstrate that each of us can leave a lasting legacy within our organizations or within our families and among friends. What will be yours?

Courageous Acts Come from Belief in Oneself

Before her funeral, Rosa Parks lay in state in the U.S. Capitol building's rotunda. More than half a century ago, this soft-spoken woman showed the world the meaning of courage and how that courage would eventually set into motion a series of world events that changed the course of history.

Looking back on her actions, Rosa Parks demonstrated how to leave a lasting legacy through her courageous acts. That day on the bus became a Rosa Parks Initiative. Her act of courage was small, but it was a powerful and high-impact moment in time. It was a turning point in all of our lives. Becoming your own mentor is about turning something around in your life. It's all about taking initiative and being self-directed.

You may say, "Well, I'm not a civil rights leader, nor am I a Rosa Parks," but neither was the Rosa we celebrate today until *after* she took a stand and did what she did. She could have moved to the back of the bus. But she didn't. She could have let that moment in time slip away. She did not. She could have lost the opportunity to grab hold and make her point that enough was enough—that she'd had it—but there was no straddling the line here. It was her time to act, and she did.

What Rosa Parks–type initiatives can you think of that make great examples of acting courageously when we are called to do so? Ask your employees what they think. Ask your kids how they feel about this, too. Discuss the issue with friends and co-workers. Write down your thoughts here:

_____

_____

_____

_____

If you are destined to achieve your greater potential when it comes to career and personal success, then you must take more Rosa Parks Initiatives in life, confront your fears and challenges, and make tough choices when called to do so.

Establish Platinum Standards That Reflect the Best in You

When you establish and live by your highest standards, like Rosa Parks did, you honor what you stand for and believe in. "Stand for something or fall for anything" is how the saying goes. Your standards by which you live and conduct your life are yours and yours alone. Make a list of personal Platinum Standards here that reflect the best in you. To get you started, here are a few examples from some of my workshop attendees in Philadelphia. Perhaps some of their Platinum Standards will help jog your own thinking.

- I define myself by who I am, not by what I have.
- I place great value on my time and my energy.
- I don't let self-defeating behaviors chip away at my goals.
- I choose abundance over self-deprivation.
- I surround myself with people I am proud of.
- I believe I am responsible for utilizing my talents and potential whenever possible.
- I give my respect and trust to others and expect the same in return.

TRICKS OF THE TRADE **Think of the Workplace As a Bureau of Tourism**
Dirk Voss is a highly regarded consultant in governmental relations and strategic organizational management. He also serves as a Code Compliance Manager for the City of Oxnard Police Department. Voss implements a unique business approach on the job. He tells people to think of their workplace, regardless of their industry, as a bureau of tourism. Voss says that when a supervisor operates the business by taking on this focus, or theme, he or she can more easily set organizational priorities, because as a bureau of tourism the workplace priorities will automatically center around performance quality, customer services, and thereby, challenge the supervisor to continually improve every aspect of service provided. Thinking of your business as a bureau of tourism makes everyone focus on the importance of serving others.

- I make choices that are in alignment with my Platinum Standards of behavior.
- I shift my paradigms upward and do not compromise downward.

Now, after you've made your own list of Platinum Standards, go back and question each one with, "How do I prove it?" By answering this question for each standard you have listed, you will be holding yourself accountable for taking action and truly living by these standards in your daily life. This is important because without action the list is meaningless.

Be Accountable for Your Choices—Each One Represents Your Intellect and Self-Esteem

You are where you are because of the choices you have made up to this point. Some folks may not want to believe this, but with the exception of very young children or those without the mental competency to make their own choices, this rule of thumb is quite accurate.

The important choices that you make and that shape your life contribute directly to either the positive or the negative ways that you handle situations on the job or personal matters at home.

> **Key Term**
>
> **Locus of Control** Locus of control is the perceived source of control over our behavior. People with internal locus of control believe that the choices they make directly impact and contribute to their destiny. These people typically have a healthy self-esteem. Those with external locus of control see themselves as victims of their circumstances and often suffer from low self-esteem.

Throughout our lives we make certain choices that help us to build up resilience that enables us to cope with life's challenges.

Did you know that whenever you make critical choices you tell the world how you see yourself? Well, you do.

Whether those choices are good or bad, right or wrong, they are the life choices you are making at that point in time. A choice may begin in your heart or in your gut, but it is in your brain where the choices you ultimately make are activated and take place.

The choices you make can empower or energize you, or they can render you helpless and defeated. If you are going to start acting as your own life coach, then it's important that you understand this concept. You also should understand that your self-confidence is directly related to what I call *choice intelligence*. The following section explains why.

What's Your CQ?

Each of us is the product of our choice-making intelligence. I like to call this CQ, or choice quotient. The process goes something like this: It all starts with our self-esteem, or self-worth. From this vantage point is where we make our life choices.

If we are feeling low about ourselves, we can make low or poor decisions and attract people who are not right for us. If we are feeling confident and good about ourselves, we tend to make better choices and attract better circumstances and people as well. The choices we make are not accidental but rather reflect our choice intelligence, which activates our minds. Our intellect helps us to choose whether or not we take the high road or the low road in our decision making.

I refer to this as intelligence in action, and it has nothing to do with a person's IQ or how high you scored on your SATs. Our self-worth is simply part of that same intelligence in action, shaping our greater potential and happiness in life.

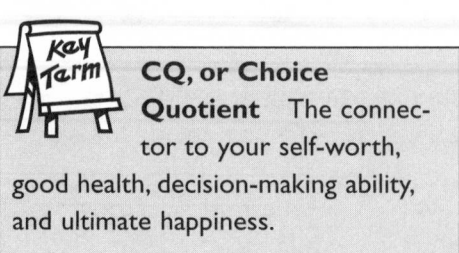

CQ, or Choice Quotient The connector to your self-worth, good health, decision-making ability, and ultimate happiness.

Later on in this book, I will illustrate for you how intelligence in action works. It's fascinating and very powerful once you grasp the concept and begin using it.

Your CQ, or choice quotient, is sacred. When you make good choices, you become a cocreator with a higher source of energy and power in deciding your future. When you don't make good choices, you end up giving away pieces of yourself, a little at a time. Be aware that this can discount your overall worth in a hurry.

Did you know that you actually encode into every cell in your body the things that you think or believe about yourself? This can be measured and has been documented in science for many years. You cannot separate your brain from your body. Consciousness is not just in the head. Therefore you will always attract what you feel worthy of, never allowing yourself to have more happiness, wealth, or success than you believe you deserve. So that poses the question, "Are you living your most abundant life?" As your own mentor, you'll have a chance to address this later in the book.

Fast Assessment of Your Present Life-Coaching Toolkit

Here's what I want you to do. Make a list right now of all the life-coaching tools you've accumulated in the past year or two. What are they? Be specific. Think of books, certifications, seminars you've attended, a coach you actually worked with on the job or privately, helpful colleagues and friends, relationships with subject matter experts, family experiences and relations in your area of expertise, a higher degree, old mentors, new mentors, professional development, personal growth, spiritual growth, physical makeovers, a new exercise plan, new family, new church, new city, life adventures, and any other life-coaching tools you have acquired. Write them down.

_____

_____

_____

All of these things and people in your life are both a conscious and subconscious part of your current life-coaching toolkit, expertise that you draw upon every day. By listing all of

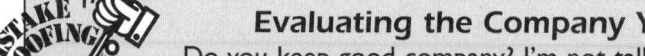

Evaluating the Company You Keep

Do you keep good company? I'm not talking about a person's social status, financial wealth, or physical attractiveness. Your inner circle speaks volumes about the kind of person you are. The people in your inner circle reflect your confidence level and self-worth in many respects. So be keenly aware of those with whom you surround yourself.

When we are kids our parents often tell us that we are judged by the company we keep and the company we choose *not* to keep. When we become adults we quickly see the truth in this message. Do the people you surround yourself with expect you to live your higher truth and support you in good times and bad? Are they fiercely loyal? Do they tolerate other people's differences? Are they generous, loving, and compassionate? Are they like-minded when it comes to how they live and work and treat others?

Even if you find your list of true friends to be quite small, remember that it's better to have 10 real friendships than a thousand apparent friends who don't support your quest or mirror your core values and work ethic.

these things and people before starting this book, you gauge where you are now and how far you've come. You'll feel a sense of what has worked for you in the past and what is not working for you now, or who is not working out with you in your life now. You'll get a good feel for what and who mean the most to you and how valuable they are to you.

By taking stock of all the tools in your toolkit that you've had to your avail over the past months, you gain greater appreciation for them and you can begin to think about how all of this might just fit into your new plan for the future. All that you have accumulated up to this point is your personal treasure chest of goodies. Some you use often and others you take out and polish only for special occasions. It doesn't matter. You decide what stays, what goes, or what you will share with those who follow in your footsteps and whom you might mentor in the future.

Your Four-Part Formula for Success Starts Here

I invite you to connect, or perhaps reconnect is a better word, with me and with this book I am so passionate about bringing to you—*Be Your Own Mentor.*

For this book, and for you, I have drawn from hundreds of workshops and seminars I have conducted worldwide. I've distilled my experience into a series of provocative self-assessments, worksheets, checklists, and exercises. In today's work environment, especially corporate America, it is easy to get derailed, consumed with ego, and even internally alienated from our greater purpose and goals. Any one of us can get caught up in the fast pace of life where we neglect to ask ourselves, "What am I doing?" "Where am I going?" "What do I really want?" Now, more than ever, as our world becomes more visibly entwined and interconnected, we need to reassess who we are and where we stand. This process begins with a distinct four-part formula and its individual action steps:

Part 1. Free Yourself!
Action Step: Get Ready to Join the Ranks of Free Agent Globalization
Part 2. Think for Yourself!
Action Step: Become an Entrepreneurial Thinker—Even If You Work for Someone Else
Part 3. Reinvent Yourself!
Action Step: Manifest Your Career and Personal Life Goals
Part 4. Ignite Yourself!
Action Step: Ignite Your Many Intelligences and Start Applying Them to Your Career—Now!

A New and Exciting Approach for Managers

This book offers you, today's manager, a new and exciting approach to career planning and personal development. It's an approach that will allow you to become your own mentor and in the process gain sharper insights to greater career and personal success. It's time to let go of yesterday's excuses, outdated beliefs, and self-imposed limitations.

If you're serious about becoming your own mentor and if you're truly tired of mediocrity and being frustrated with the direction in which your life is moving, then don't tolerate one more day of the same old thing. Get ready to clear the slate and try something new, relevant and powerful, fun and intriguing.

And what's expected of you? Only that you willingly go forward with the genuine desire to develop those parts of yourself that are yearning to be expressed. You get to choose. Pick the parts of this book that fit your lifestyle best. The lessons in this book are yours for the asking and yours for the taking. You select what actions you will take and what behaviors you will engage in. Whatever you decide, simply know that there is no grander contribution that you can make to this world than achieving your greater potential, sharpening your competencies, and honing your natural talents.

I hope you'll be so excited to start this program that you'll jump out of bed every morning ready to read a page or two and start this self-transforming process with zeal and gusto. If you do, you won't be sorry.

Imagine a world where you are guided to be your most authentic self, a world where you can be your own mentor and measure your many successes, big and small, in short order. Contemplate for a moment what a different world it might, indeed, be. Now let's get started.

Part 1

Free Yourself!

Action Step: Get Ready to Join the Ranks of Free Agent Globalization

Do-It-Yourself Life-Coaching Formula for Becoming Your Own Mentor

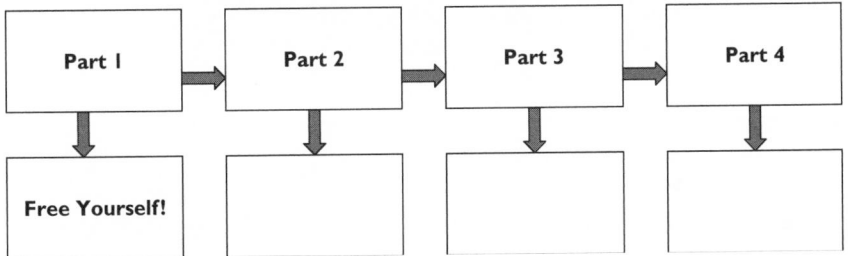

Traditional Career Planning Will Be Gone As We Know It

Get Ready to Join the Ranks of Free Agent Globalization!

Welcome to the world of free agent globalization. Say good-bye to the one-size-fits-all career-pathing mentality and to all its endless boundaries. Instead, say hello to business on Planet Earth—no longer as we've come to know it—business that grows and operates organically, without traditional, linear career planning, business that is chuck full of unlimited potential. It's a very exciting time to be a part of the work world. Are you ready to embrace the future, here and now?

What Does the Term *Free Agent* Mean?

More than a decade ago, former White House speechwriter and author Daniel Pink brilliantly wrote about America's new independent work group and how they were transforming the way we live. He called the group free agents. Pink wrote the popular book *Free Agent Nation: The Future of Working for Yourself* (Warner Business Books) and soon became a leading authority on what's also known as a free agent nation, or free agent USA. The theme of working for oneself ties in strongly with the message of this book and how to successfully become your own mentor. (In Part 2, I'll address more specifically how to become an entrepreneurial thinker and free agent even if you work for someone else.) To be a free agent is not just something that happens in the United States, not by a long stretch. This is why I coined the term *free agent globalization* for this book. Every free agent out there is truly a global phenomenon in his or her own right. I think you'll see what I mean as you read on.

A free agent is considered a soloist in the truest sense. This is someone who works for himself or herself. For thousands of years soloists have worked for themselves as painters, actors, writers, designers, scientists, clergy, and other professionals, hopping from project to project. As time went on, they became better known as freelancers or, as they are sometimes called today, e-lancers. They are Internet-savvy workers who use high-speed, mobile technology to further their careers and lifestyles.

Free agent globalization represents innovative workers who mentor themselves to do things their way and in their timeframe, yet they get the job done with extraordinary pride, quality, zero defects, a myriad of intelligences, and grand exuberance.

Free agent globalization does not accept a world full of outdated work customs and social mores that too often collapse under the weight of their own absurdity and hypocrisy. Whether it's the strange office politics of employees who don't pull their own weight or managers who fail to lead with integrity, free agents have cut themselves loose from the environment of organizational dysfunction. Their belief is that most people do want to work hard and do a great job for others and at the

Free Agent A free agent is an economic icon of the twenty-first century. Free agents are techno-savvy and often work from home or "third spaces," such as FedEx, Kinko's, Starbucks, or high-tech–equipped airport lounges. They are more than 35 million strong in the United States alone. Worldwide statistics on free agents are difficult to nail down, and global mapmakers have yet to give free agents official locations. As domestic and international telecommuting increases, as our global society gets smaller and smaller due to the Internet, and as business trends and services expand internationally, tracking free agents becomes more difficult.

Typically, free agents were thought to be in their 20s or 30s—free spirits in the workforce, never hesitating to move from one job to another or even jump from one career to another when the urge would strike. However, we know now that there is no age limit to a free agent and that many free agents in the world today are in their 40s, 50s, 60s, 70s, and 80s!

A free agent may be the VP of Talent at a Fortune 500 company one year and backpacking in the Himalayas the next. The mentality of the free agent—and there is such a free agent mentality—is that life is too short to spend all in one spot and that job security is a superstition. Free agents won't commit their loyalty to one company easily, but only if their values and personal needs are being respected and met.

same time those same people are utterly turned off by useless distractions going on within companies that lead to much ado about nothing.

If you adopt the practices of free agent globalization as your own, then you agree that it's time for new terms and new ways of doing business in this world. You take on the responsibility of being your own mentor and not relying on one outside organization. You get it when I say, "Eight clients are better than one boss!"

The message is simple. Working in a free agent global society is very personal and direct, and people just like you can and do strike harmony between who they are and what they do for a living, and as a result, great benefits are realized by those for whom they are working, whether they are working independently or for someone else.

Can a Manager Be a Free Agent within a Corporation?

Tens of million of managers, supervisors, and employees world-wide have decided to do their own thing. They've decided to work and behave like free agents or what's often referred to as a new and extremely intelligent breed of not only the self-employed, but includes the self-directed and accountable self-initiators who do work within the confines of certain organizations. So a key question is this: Can a manager or employee really be a free agent within a corporation? The answer is yes! Remember, at their core, a free agent is simply a breed of worker who places very few limits on boundaries and has a great distaste for traditional work environments. Are there organizations who play to that mentality and, thereby, create a free agent globalization environment? Google anyone?

Free Agent *Employee* Is No Longer an Oxymoron

As you can see from the Google smart managing example, yes, there are lots of free agent *employees* out there too. If you can find, or create the right free agent globalization environment, then you too can act as your own free agent and still work for a large, or small, organization.

If you're the kind of worker who is always seeking out the next cool assignment in your company, or navigating your career path with boundaryless opportunity and zeal, then even if you're getting a W-2 form at the end of the year instead of a 1099-Misc. form, you're still mentoring yourself and thinking like a free agent. That's the spirit!

Good-Bye to Traditional Career Planning

Do you remember the days of traditional career counseling and planning? You're probably thinking right about now, "Oh, no, is she getting ready to tell me to kiss this concept good-bye too?"

The Closest Thing to Being a Free Agent in a Global Organization—Work for Google!

Smart Managing

Google gets it! They know that in order to attract and retain brilliant people, they've got to create a free agent globalization environment for them to work in. Did you know that at the world's most successful search engine company, located in Mountain View, California, engineers are encouraged to spend 20 percent of their time working on independent projects of their choice? No wonder Google gets almost 1,500 resumes a day!

In addition, fueling the quality of life while at work is another Google trademark. Here are just a few of their quality-of-life perks:

- $30 massages
- Free onsite washers and dryers with free detergent to do your laundry
- Onsite car washes
- Onsite notaries
- Free flu shots
- Free onsite physicians
- 11 free cafes and lots of gourmet meals
- Haircuts
- International language classes
- Gyms, lap pools, volleyball courts, and game rooms
- All-expenses paid ski trips
- $2,000 bonuses for new hire referrals
- Free shuttle services to pick up and drop off employees in the Bay area
- Dry cleaning drop-off
- Oil change facility
- $5,000 to be environmentally healthy and buy a hybrid car

Sound like a free agent globablization organization? You bet!

Smart Managing

Code Enforcement Manager by Day, Restaurateur by Night

I first met Rob Silverstein when he attended a leadership workshop I was teaching at a national conference for code enforcement officers in Las Vegas, Nevada. Now a friend, Rob still shows up at my seminars with his natural enthusiasm and free-agent spirit. Rob is the perfect example of why a free-agent employee is no longer an oxymoron in today's workplace. In addition to being an inspirational leader to his team as a senior code compliance officer at the City of Oxnard's Fire Department, Rob and his brother Joe decided to start JRS Investment Group, specializing in restaurant investments, among others. At one of their popular steakhouses, Dakota's, in Westlake Village, California, Rob and his wife Shane hosted my daughter, Autumn, and me for a blow-out meal, complete with out-of-this-world service and attention to detail! It was in this environment where I immediately detected the same competencies, talents, skills, and personality Rob uses on the job for the City of Oxnard. However, this night his skills were being transferred to employees and business partners in this fun restaurant environment. Among the great employees and servers that evening, I focused primarily on our superstar-server Dana Sax and wine connoisseur Chris Kim. Both were quite noticeably treated by Rob and Dakota's owner Adam Stern, not just like family, but like shareholders and owners! The pride was palpable and the steaks divine!

Tricks of the Trade

These Tricks of the Trade Build Free Agent Morale in Lots of Creative Companies:

- Telecommuting for employees
- Allowing job switching
- Flex hours for employees
- Bringing pets to work
- Bringing kids to work
- Encouraging personal growth and development
- Encouraging career growth and development
- Longer vacation time
- Having fun
- Feeding employees good food—for free

Well, yes, actually I am. If you want to be your own mentor, then you've got to let go of the old ways in which we all planned our careers. It went something like this.

It started with whatever education you had, and was then followed by at least 20 or 30 years of hard work in one organiza-

> **Free Agent Employee or Free Agent Manager or Supervisor** The terms free agent employee or free agent manager, or supervisor, are no longer considered oxymorons ready to join the ranks of contradictory terms, such as mandatory option, jumbo shrimp, pretty ugly, tax return, personal computer, healthy tan, and work party!

tion, maybe two, and that was later followed by retirement. Oh, and by the way, the career choices we pursued were limited to what we studied in school. If you studied education, you became a teacher, even if you hated it. If you studied law, you became a lawyer, even if you hated that too. Is it any wonder that almost 80 percent of the working population claim to dislike their jobs, and to sit in extreme boredom? I'm not saying that career planning is going to become one chaotic event of folks careening from one job to another, but traditional career planning as we know it is over. Welcome to the future.

The Future of Career Planning

You probably noticed earlier that I use the word "pathing." I like the sound of *career pathing* more than I do *career planning*. Why? Because the word *path* implies both a road to somewhere and the ultimate destination, where that road might lead you. In other words, career pathing of the future will have fewer boundaries and planning restrictions and instead will be filled with more creative opportunities that grow organically rather than in a linear and systematic fashion.

How we plan our future careers today is really more an issue of how we choose to evolve over time. Our evolving into our future careers is based upon a cumulative repertoire

> **Key Term**
>
> **Portfolio Careers** Portfolio careers transcend the boundaries of what defines traditional career planning. Portfolio careers are careers that *evolve* based on a person's skills, competencies, life experiences, education, and knowledge. They grow naturally from evolving economic times, world trends and discoveries, and new inventions and are primarily driven by mobile technologies. Portfolio careers continually morph and result in new and better career opportunities that may have never even existed before. For example, mobile technology has organically, or quite naturally, created new and improved business opportunities in the fields of music, medicine, television and radio, advertising, and public relations. Portfolio careers spring up when you least expect them to and continue to evolve to meet our changing global economy and the fast-paced world we live in.

of competencies, skills, experience, know-how, and education applied to a collection of diversified roles over a period of time. The term sometimes used for this is *portfolio careers*.

Career Development Requires Boundaryless Careers and Boundaryless Thinking

The typical boundaryless career is characterized by a career identity that is independent of the employer. For example, a free agent simply says, "I am a software engineer." He or she does not say, "I am a software engineer for XYZ software company, working in department A." The boundaryless career is one that allows a free agent to combine knowledge, flexibility, innovation, and efficiency to enhance the quality of the free agent's work. The boundaryless career also includes the business networks that are independent of specific firms, even specific industries. The boundaryless career and its business networks all work together seamlessly.

How Did We Arrive Here?

Global competition, along with organizational restructuring, has revolutionized career planning as we once knew it. This movement has destroyed the traditional blueprint, or career mapping and career counseling. Self-mentors appreciate that we live in a new organizational era where worker mobility and freedom have become the two most important connections between workers and the firms they contract with around the world. It is at the convergence of where mobility meets freedom that a primary shift in attitude takes place between climbing the traditional organizational ladder and a boundaryless career mentality.

Assessing Your Boundaryless-Thinking Aptitude Start here, by first exploring whether or not you are a boundaryless thinker, a

A Metaphor for Boundaryless Careers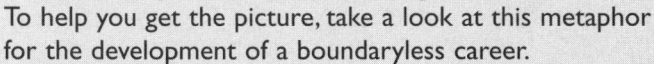

To help you get the picture, take a look at this metaphor **TOOLS** for the development of a boundaryless career.

Think of your career life span as a set of building blocks, the kind you used to play with as a kid. Each block represents your skills, your business connections, special interests and competencies, education, specialized training, and other valuable attributes and relationships that you possess. How have you used these building blocks so far? Is the structure you've built with them something strong and secure, or wobbly and boring? Okay, here's the shift in thinking. We used to think we were stuck with what we built with our career building blocks. But boundaryless career thinking tells us that we can easily dismantle whatever structure we've built and build something new and more interesting. We can experiment with odd combinations, knowing that these combinations are, indeed, endless.

Think of the building block approach this way: you are actually refashioning your career style and purpose. The point is this. The traditional corporate or governmental ladder approach to building our careers is over. But the building block approach offers infinite possibilities, especially if you are willing to act as your own mentor. It's an approach made for do-it-yourselfers, like you.

requisite for any boundaryless career leap. Embracing this concept will also help you to better understand and later apply the Mentoring Compass you'll be using in Chapter 3.

Take this self-assessment and see where you stand.

In each description listed in this assessment, circle the number that best matches how you see yourself when it comes to boundaryless thinking in your career choices. The higher the numbers you circle, the greater the indication that you are a boundaryless thinker and may be ready to step outside the box of traditional career planning. Lower numbers indicate areas for additional focus and improvement, consideration, and solution-based thinking. They also may indicate that a boundaryless career path may not be right for you at this time.

Are You Ready to Break Free of One-Size-Fits-All Career Planning?

Boundaryless-Thinking Self-Assessment Snapshot

1. I am ready to free myself from these ties that bind me on the job! And it's not because I am trying to hide or flee a traditional work environment and its policies. It's just not for me anymore. I've grown organically in my career and want to take the leap of faith. I'm ready to join the legion of free agents and make my own way. I want to be a knight for hire! I am a boundaryless thinker and I want to apply this aptitude in my new career life.

   Not for me! 1 2 3 4 5 6 7 8 9 10 Sounds just like me!

2. I am reading this book so that I can be my own mentor. I am ready to take on the "do-it-yourself" approach to achieving greater career and personal success in my life. I'm committed to doing less talking and taking more action!

   Not for me! 1 2 3 4 5 6 7 8 9 10 Sounds just like me!

3. I'm not afraid of making mistakes. After all, it's part of life's growth process. I try to always learn from my mistakes and share them with others so that the same mistakes won't be repeated and cost someone else pain or loss. I've learned not to be afraid to show my human side and foibles. I believe failure is a school where the greatest lessons in life often take place.

   Not for me! 1 2 3 4 5 6 7 8 9 10 Sounds just like me!

4. I enjoy multitasking. I can spin a lot of plates and not drop any of them 99 percent of the time. I am pretty good at prioritizing things and accomplishing the objectives of a project. I have a sense of what's most important and I put those things first. I don't get easily distracted, and when I do, I can get back on track fast.

   Not for me! 1 2 3 4 5 6 7 8 9 10 Sounds just like me!

5. I am not hung up on money or security issues. I don't go to work counting the days until I collect my pension. I don't rely on anyone or any organization to take care of me and my family for life. I expect things will change and change drastically. I'm ready when they do. I don't equate change with loss.

   Not for me! 1 2 3 4 5 6 7 8 9 10 Sounds just like me!

6. I crave spontaneity! I am extremely flexible and like to mix things up. I'm easily bored with everyday routines. I want to be challenged and reach for the stars!

   Not for me! 1 2 3 4 5 6 7 8 9 10 Sounds just like me!

7. I feel empowered when I get to make life-changing choices. I like it when others trust my judgment and let me take the lead. I feel strongly about my expertise and like to share my advice and experience with those who will listen. Approval from others is not something I think about. I have confidence in myself, and when I am unsure, I know who to go to or where to find the answers fast.

   Not for me! 1 2 3 4 5 6 7 8 9 10 Sounds just like me!

(continued)

8. I would really like to join the ranks of free agent globalization. I believe in the concept. It makes good sense to me given the global trends of organizations and workers everywhere. I want to be a part of this, and soon. I'm so glad I bought this book!

Not for me! 1 2 3 4 5 6 7 8 9 10 Sounds just like me!

9. I have more energy than an atom! I use a myriad of mobile technology gadgets to get things done and make fast decisions. I can respond with urgency to an emergency and keep an energetic pace comfortable for others to join in and give me their feedback. I am fast to get back to people and get moving on projects. I don't drag my feet. I'm an active participant, not just an observer from the sidelines.

Not for me! 1 2 3 4 5 6 7 8 9 10 Sounds just like me!

10. I like the building block approach to creating a boundaryless career. After all, I always did like playing with Legos as a kid. I'm not about well-defined structure. In fact, I enjoy taking on roles and opportunities that are not necessarily set in stone and rigidly structured. I want to disassemble my boring career and rebuild it all with my new attitude and this approach.

Not for me! 1 2 3 4 5 6 7 8 9 10 Sounds just like me!

11. I consider myself my most reliable mentor. I have other mentors I draw from when necessary, but on a day-to-day basis, I am my own best life coach and mentor. I am a self-starter and self-directed person, as well as an intentional learner.

Not for me! 1 2 3 4 5 6 7 8 9 10 Sounds just like me!

12. I believe it is up to me to continue my learning patterns in life. It's not the organization's job or somebody else's responsibility to keep me growing. After college is when the learning really begins and I enjoy online research, advanced classes, attending conferences, and continually upgrading my performance. I tap into the resources I can afford, and when I can't afford them I use free resources and affordable learning methods available on the Internet or through other venues.

Not for me! 1 2 3 4 5 6 7 8 9 10 Sounds just like me!

13. I consider myself a risk taker, but not a reckless risk taker. I first evaluate the situation and calculate the risks involved. I take an entrepreneurial approach to things, even if I work for someone else. I consider it my responsibility to do so.

    Not for me! 1 2 3 4 5 6 7 8 9 10 Sounds just like me!

14. I refuse to let fear get in my way. I can identify my fears and work to overcome them. I know they hold no power over me whatsoever and I continually remind myself of this. I confront my fears and anxieties head on and take on projects even when I am afraid to do so, knowing that my competencies will get me through.

    Not for me! 1 2 3 4 5 6 7 8 9 10 Sounds just like me!

15. I consider myself fully accountable for the choices I make and the actions I take.

    Not for me! 1 2 3 4 5 6 7 8 9 10 Sounds just like me!

16. I am ready for an extreme life-coaching makeover! I see opportunity in projects that allow me to think outside the box, or even blow up the box! I'm ready to use this book and other resources to help me set the stage for action and change in my life.

    Not for me! 1 2 3 4 5 6 7 8 9 10 Sounds just like me!

17. I am courageous. I am a leader and a thinker. I am a real-world mentor who navigates toward courage and hope in the face of the unexpected and in the most difficult of times.

    Not for me! 1 2 3 4 5 6 7 8 9 10 Sounds just like me!

18. I stand for something. I look within myself for answers and hold myself accountable for my actions and decisions. I am proud of who I am and what I do. I know that what I do for a living does not define who I am as a person. I can separate the two. I behave in a way that is consistent with how I see myself and I hold myself accountable to living in alignment with my Platinum Standards I listed earlier in this book.

    Not for me! 1 2 3 4 5 6 7 8 9 10 Sounds just like me!

Record here specific areas you would like to focus on and work toward. List your ideas here and plan to readdress them as you move through this book and program.

Set dates for completion and take time to revisit statements in this self-assessment that require additional concentration and deeper thinking.

Manager's Checklist for Chapter 1

❏ Portfolio careers transcend the boundaries of what defines traditional career planning. They grow naturally from evolving economic times, world trends and discoveries, and new inventions and are primarily driven by mobile technologies.

❏ Having a career *path* implies both a road to somewhere and the ultimate destination of where that road might lead you.

❏ Boundaryless careers require boundaryless thinking. It's important to look at these careers as you would building blocks, where the opportunities for what you build, dismantle, and then build again are endless.

❏ Free agent globalization will continue to morph the way millions of people choose to work and grow their careers. It will require an entrepreneurial mindset and risk-taking mentality, unlike at any other time in history.

Designing Your Best Life

No, You Can't Be Anything You Want to Be

This is an important chapter in learning how to be your own mentor. It's important because this chapter becomes the voice of reason and reality early on for all that you do from this point forward when implementing and applying the lessons of this life-coaching program. I like to think of it as a program that prepares you, the reader, for your most authentic self and your greatest successes, all while helping you to accept and appreciate deep down what might *not* be your reality, no matter how much you dream about it or want it.

Embrace Your Reality

Understanding that we cannot be anything we want to be is an important lesson for all of us to learn. When we grasp this concept, it opens up an infinite number of doors and horizons for us to become all that we are truly capable of becoming. That is an enormous proposition, and it is very exciting! As your own mentor, you will be learning in this chapter how to calibrate the

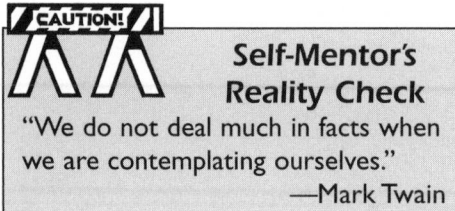

Self-Mentor's Reality Check

"We do not deal much in facts when we are contemplating ourselves."
—Mark Twain

many compasses within your natural inner guidance system—compasses that will lead you to your greater capabilities, talents, and competencies—all of which will ultimately guide you to achieving your greater career and personal success, as suggested in the title of this book.

People's Expectations of Us

When we were children, many of us were told that we could be anything we wanted to be. If you believed in something strongly enough, we were told, then it could happen for you. In addition to this, growing up we were often surrounded by other people's expectations of us, and those expectations might have little or nothing to do with who we are or what we might be capable of becoming in life.

So maybe your great Aunt Hilda, who had the best intentions at the time, told you that you were the most handsome and smartest little scientist in the family, but if science isn't one of your basic core competencies, talents, and passions,

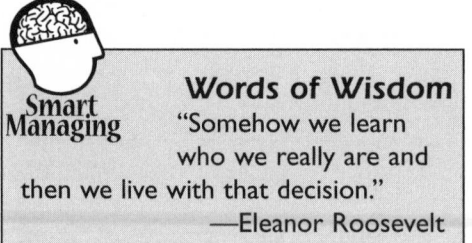

Smart Managing

Words of Wisdom

"Somehow we learn who we really are and then we live with that decision."
—Eleanor Roosevelt

then you probably won't wind up winning a Nobel Prize in Science, or even end up playing a crucial role in Mrs. Stevens's seventh-grade class science project.

Accepting What's *Not* Right for You Is a Gift

If your real gifts and competencies had all of your inner compass needles pointed toward careers as a famous artist, ballet dancer, or Pulitzer Prize–winning author, the science gig may not have worked out as Aunt Hilda imagined. That's a good thing—a very good thing. Realizing up front and accepting what is *not* right for us in this world is just as valuable as discovering what we are truly great at and what we can bring to our careers and relationships with unbridled passion. When we pursue what we are good at or capable of learning, we excel. We exhibit greater confidence and a stronger self-image, and we live in a much happier world. Sounds good, doesn't it?

It takes time and soul-searching to evaluate our competencies so that we can be our most authentic selves and expand upon what we know to be true and right for us as individuals. It takes strength of character like that of the fictional, but inspirational, Betty Suarez.

Making Ugly Pretty

A popular television program called *Ugly Betty*, starring America Ferrera, has become the real-world voice of reason and a gut reality check for job seekers and fans alike, not only in the United States, but also, through translated versions, in Mexico, India, Russia, and Germany. The power of this television show's message is unprecedented, because it deals with accepting our reality, accepting ourselves as we truly are and are meant to be.

The star of the show, Ugly Betty, as she is known by loyal viewers, has always wanted to make it in the publishing arena of high fashion and especially wants to land a job at tony *Mode* magazine in Manhattan. As a promising college graduate from a struggling Latino family in Queens, Betty was promptly rejected at her first job interview at Meade Publications. Her rejection was based solely on her appearance (thus the series' title). And so, though Betty possesses a strong work ethic and is extremely productive and clever, her dreams to work at the superficial and snooty workplace are always overshadowed by the fact that she isn't the best-looking woman in New York.

Sure, Betty is sweet, hardworking, and extremely qualified,

but let's face it: she doesn't fit the typical employee look at *Mode* magazine. Unlike all of her future co-workers, Betty isn't tall, thin, beautiful, botoxed, nipped, tucked, and implanted. But she doesn't want to be, either. She knows who she is and what she's great at. She's her own mentor in a world where mentors for her "type" don't make themselves easily available. (Fast forward: Being her own mentor is what eventually takes Betty to the top, making her one of the most valued workers at *Mode* and eventually sought after by another popular fashion publication. Okay, rewind.)

Never failing to be true to herself, Betty has always had one "realistic" goal in life, to make it into New York's fashion publishing business, and *Mode* is her shot at it all. I didn't say she wanted to be a high-fashion model. She'd never make the cut by fashion photographers or runway modeling standards, and she knows it, and she doesn't waste her time trying to be something she is not. Betty Suarez knows her strengths and her weaknesses, and she plays her strengths and competencies to the hilt, never compromising her preference for out-of-style fashion accessories—enter the ugliest poncho on the face of the earth—or a mouth full of metal braces, eyeglasses in lieu of contacts, and a hairstyle from 1975.

A Pop Icon Speaks

"I will not sell cures.... I did not see Elvis.... The truth is not out there.... I will never win an Emmy."

—Bart Simpson

Ever Feel Like a Fish Out of Water?

Have you ever felt like an Ugly Betty or an Ugly Bob? A fish out of water? Someone who didn't fit in? Did you cut bait and run, or did you find your greatest competencies and apply them to the job of your dreams anyway, not trying to be someone or act like something you are not?

That's what Betty does (after all, she's her own best coach and mentor) and ultimately winds up as the assistant to *Mode*'s executive editor Daniel Meade, played by Eric Mabius, where her uniqueness, strength of character, unshallowness, and intelligent approach to running a fashion publication pay off. Reluctant to hire her at first, Daniel begins to appreciate her can-do spirit and hot fashion ideas. She never tries to present herself as one of the "beautiful people" (which she isn't); instead, she presents herself as just one of the most "effective, nurturing, bright, creative, and highly tolerant people" *Mode* ever employed (which she is).

The two become a formidable pair and soon take the fashion industry by storm, using their greatest competencies and not following in the traditional footsteps of those who came before them.

Are you ready to take your chosen profession by storm and design your best life? If the answer is yes, then it's time to start using the multitude of self-mentoring compasses that lie within you.

Snap Out of It!

As your own mentor, you must be honest with yourself. Start by listening to the voice within about what it is you'll be spending your life doing. Avoid wasting time and heartache listening to what others may want you to be or believe you should be doing, and start by acknowledging right up front where you are on the learning curve relative to what you really can become and what you plan to do with your life.

For example, let's say that you've always dreamed of becoming a NASA astronaut. Okay, but you're 55 years old. You don't have a pilot's license and can't get one because you have serious health complications. Well, then, no matter how much you want to be in this role, or how often others tell you that you can do it in the face of all odds, the reality is this: you most likely will not meet the minimum requirements necessary to become an astronaut for NASA, nor will you find yourself flying the space shuttle, or any other space vehicle, for that matter, anytime soon. That's just the reality of your competencies.

Snap Out of It!

In the hit 1987 movie *Moonstruck*, when Ronnie Cammareri, played by Nicolas Cage, professes his unlikely love for Loretta Castorini, played by Cher, after she cooks him a steak in his apartment, Loretta slaps Ronnie and yells, "Snap out of it!" Sometimes we have to snap out of it, too.

Successful self-mentors set themselves up for success, not disappointment. They do this by excavating their strongest, most genuine interests and talents, without regard to what their parents or best friends tell them they are good at. You'll need to identify your emotional and intellectual competencies as they relate to achieving your greatest personal and business success. After you examine these things, it will be time to ask this question: *Is this dream at all realistic for me to achieve?* If the answer is yes, after you have evaluated your competencies and have answered a series of self-assessment questions, then the sky may very well be the limit!

Don't Blow It!
Denying your inner truth and authenticity is like trying to keep the lid on a pressure cooker that has built up too much steam. You can try as much as you like, but containing all that built-up steam will be next to impossible—something's going to blow!

To Be Your Own Mentor, You Must Nurture Your Nature

Everything in our universe has a nature, and that nature needs to be nurtured. This implies that there are limits to everything and everyone, as well as great potential and capabilities that have yet to be discovered. If you are seeking a way to mentor yourself without first accepting and understanding the raw materials that you have to work with, what you create in life may well turn out to be fake and awkward. You cannot perform at your highest level of potential when you are behaving and acting in contradiction to how you see yourself.

Using Your Inner Guidance System

People cannot perform at high levels of productivity or performance when they behave in a manner that is inconsistent with how they see themselves.

Design a Do-It-Yourself Career and Personal Success Life Strategy

All right, you've decided to be your own mentor. Perhaps you are someone who is seeking greater personal growth and happiness. Or maybe you are a manager or supervisor, a government worker, or leader in a multinational organization based overseas. You may also be a self-employed free agent, e-lancer, consultant, entrepreneur, mompreneur, aspiring artist, or scientist with a need to reignite your passion for work and spirit.

Whoever we are or whatever our ultimate goals are, sometimes we just need guidance to get to where we are going. This book is for you, and the transformation you are

Mompreneur Mompreneurs are free agents working from home in most cases. Of course they have children, and they also have the desire to run their own businesses. Mompreneurs are innovative and serious about making money and making headway. Home-based businesses are in the tens of millions and rising worldwide, and moms are leading the way with their successful free-agent approach to careers in areas such as publishing, bookkeeping, catering, graphic arts, child care, and pet sitting. Even professional mompreneurs are hanging a shingle in their subterranean home space as lawyers, doctors, therapists, and CPAs. Mompreneurs are a subset of the microbusiness industry.

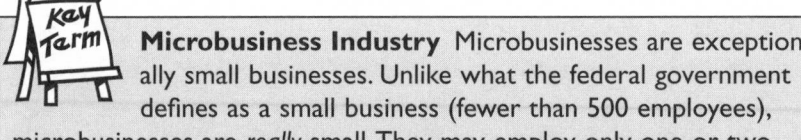

> **Microbusiness Industry** Microbusinesses are exceptionally small businesses. Unlike what the federal government defines as a small business (fewer than 500 employees), microbusinesses are *really* small. They may employ only one or two people, and those people are usually free agent freelancers, or e-lancers, mompreneurs, and consultants. They are a growing force in the development of free agent globalization everywhere. Many of these businesses have Internet storefronts. After all, isn't that how Amazon .com got started? For the most part, entry into microbusiness operations is easy. Starting a microbusiness is about as easy as getting a driver's license, or membership card at Costco or Sam's Club.

about to embark upon is an exciting one. Don't worry about your past mistakes or the poor choices you've made along the way. We've all been there, done that. That's yesterday's news.

Forget about the Past—Discover the Pearl within You and What Lies Ahead

Your life's most significant changes lie before you, not in the grit of the past. It's the grit that life throws at you, though, that becomes embedded in your work ethic and belief system over time. Just like the grain of sand that embeds itself within the oyster's shell, the grit we deal with as managers and supervisors, workers, and free agents can be transformed into an exquisite pearl when we have the tools and techniques to make new choices. The following system, which I call compasses, was designed to help you uncover and polish that one-of-a-kind pearl forming within you.

A Guidance System and Compasses to Help You Be Your Own Mentor

Did you know that you have a very sophisticated, state-of-the-art guidance system that resides within you? Well, you do. It's a guidance system that was built so that you could be your own mentor. It's organic, and grows naturally and it's sitting right inside you, waiting to be used. And now, with a little latitude, this one-of-a-kind navigational system has been refined to feature the 10 premium life compasses that will help you navigate your way to greater career and personal success.

Are You Asking Yourself the Smartest Questions?

These compasses are equipped to give you all the indications of what your strongest emotional and intellectual competencies are and how you can apply them. These compasses also inspire life-changing questions that when answered become powerful coaching tools for moving ahead.

Being your own mentor is never about having all the answers; it's about asking yourself the smartest questions you can come up with. This self-exploratory questioning process opens us up to unstoppable possibilities, new ideas, and life strategies that tie it all together. These questions bring into focus the action steps you will take to discover the real you. They also help you to dump the life excuses you may have been holding onto for so long, excuses that have kept you in "victim mode," or excuses for why you're unhappy, fearful, feeling unsuccessful, or not taking your best shot at living life fully.

If you've been feeling lost up to this point, then this section will help you to find your way back on course. You'll be glad to know that this inner guidance system is a fixed point you can count on and refer to through the years. There's no expiration date stamped on it like on the milk you buy in the grocery store.

Next, within the pages of this book, you will find a powerful course of action for becoming your own mentor and for navigating toward a smoother life journey. The tools in this book will equip you to design your best life and to mentor yourself toward a one-of-a-kind destiny.

Competency Webster's dictionary defines competency or competence as "having the possession of a required skill, qualification, or capacity; having suitable or sufficient skill, knowledge, experience, etc. for some purpose."

Activating the System

How do you really go about acting as your own mentor? How do you choose a life that expresses all that you can be? The first step is to identify your most critical human competencies. Then you'll activate the system with smart questions and introspective answers that apply only to you.

Competencies can be divided easily into two areas:

1. Emotional, human capabilities, or what are sometimes called soft-skill competencies.
2. Intellectual, practical, or hard-skill competencies.

Attribute Bundle A collection of all our competencies combined, including both emotional and intellectual, soft-skill and hard-skill abilities.

A collection of all these competencies is what is called a person's *attribute bundle*. The key here will be to identify both skill sets and then to align them to the business or personal goals and desires you are establishing while you are reading this book. Worksheets are provided to make this easier.

I am asking you to dovetail both sides of your competencies in order to mentor yourself fully and successfully. We cannot separate our emotional competencies from our intellectual competencies, no more than we can separate our professional lives from our personal lives. Remember the "whole-person" approach I spoke of earlier in the Preface of this book? I told you back then that in order to mentor yourself to a higher level of potential and competency you must also take what I call the whole-person approach to life and that by doing so you would sharpen both your emotional and intellectual competencies. This section is part of that approach. I also promised you a special magnifying glass of sorts to help you focus on and examine, close up and personal, the direction in which you are headed. The following compasses and exercises are what I was referring to.

How to Get Started

Here you will find 10 premium self-mentoring compasses. Remember, you have a sophisticated guidance system already set up within you to activate these compasses. But you might not have activated this critical navigational system yet, or you may have ignored it until now. This neglect may have been going on for months or maybe even years. It's time to activate the system by reviewing all 10 premium self-mentoring compasses. All are calibrated and pointing their needles in the direction of your life's greatest desires. All you need to do is pay close attention to the direction you're being pointed in. The action steps for all of this will come later in the book.

All 10 Compasses Are of Equal Significance—You Judge the Importance

The main graphic for this exercise is simple and straightforward. The symbol for north is evident at the top of the compass design. All of the premium self-mentoring compasses are equal in significance, but you are the one to judge the importance of each depending on where you are in your life at this time and place.

Each area of life appears at different places on the compass—north, south, east, and west—to indicate the changing directions in our lives. The compass places also indicate that sometimes we are headed in one direction, only to quickly turn and go in another direction when we least expect it.

Here's How It Works

Featured around the main compass are 10 premium self-mentoring compasses representing the primary areas of life, all capable of helping you to design your best life right now and to help you be your own creative and effective mentor. These self-mentoring compasses include the following:

- Higher Power Compass
- Health Compass
- Feeling Groovy Compass
- Money Magnet Compass
- Humanity Compass
- Abundant Living Compass
- Intelligences Compass
- Life Expander Compass
- Career and Business Compass
- The Little Miss Sunshine Phenomenon, Family, Friends, and Kids Compass

How does this tool work? It works by helping you to clarify and focus on key areas and issues going on now in your life, both professional and personal. It gives you something to relate to and refer to as you move your life forward. Again, this tool does not have an expiration date stamped on it. Its effectiveness and usability won't expire or become obsolete.

The tool is designed to help you dovetail your professional journey with your personal journey.

Answering Relevant Questions Activates Your Inner Guidance System   Another way this tool works is by featuring a key set of questions for each life area. These are exploratory self-assessment questions, and the answers to these questions will activate and unveil the truth about how you are feeling or thinking, or will supply the reason you have not taken certain action steps, or will help you to identify someone or something that is holding you back. A variety of things can surface, depending on your background and life experiences. There are no right or wrong responses. There are no grades or evaluation scores to process. Your responses simply become the perfect reflection of who you are in this moment in time and underscore what you believe to be true and applicable to you and no one else.

> **Wisdom of Winston Churchill's Leadership**
>
> **Smart Managing**
>
> "You create your own universe as you go along."
>
> —Winston Churchill

In addition, I encourage you to add on to the questions I have provided. No one knows the smartest questions to ask better than you. Remember, that's part of being your own mentor and part of activating the directional compasses in this exercise.

Start here by familiarizing yourself with this overall guidance system and the 10 premium self-mentoring compasses (see Figure 2.1 on page 52).

Take Control: Design Your Dream Life

Back in this book's Introduction, I said that when you become your own mentor, you also become the author of your life story. You are the sole navigator of your life, no one else; hence the compass graphic. Take control by examining every premium self-mentoring compass in the graphic provided and complete the accompanying worksheets and questions for each area of your life. Through this process you will begin to truly mentor yourself to your greatest level of potential and talent, uncovering your hidden desires and planning your best life from this point forward.

Sample to Follow

The sample provided was offered by one of my *Be Your Own Mentor* seminar attendees, a gentleman of about 40 years of age, who very successfully, using this tool, made major life

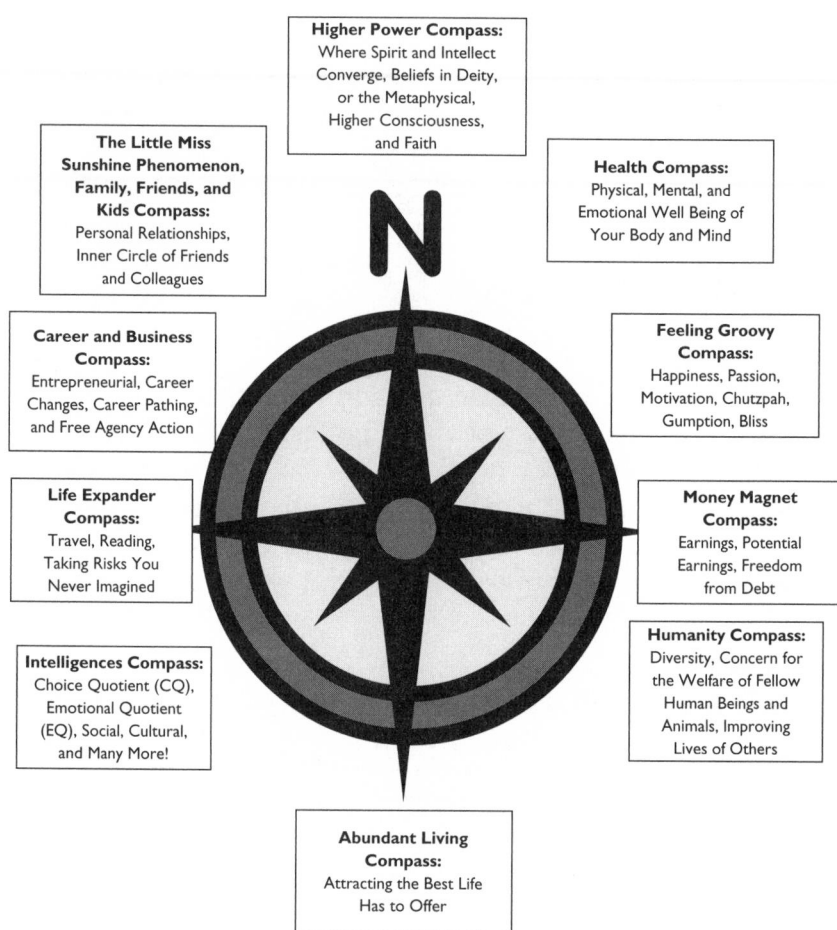

Figure 2.1.   Ten Premium Self-Mentoring Compasses

changes to his career and personal life. He wrote to me about 18 months after he attended my seminar and shared his many extraordinary life changes. His name is Larry Madison. Review Larry's approach to using these self-mentoring life compasses and then complete your own worksheets of introspection and planning.

Larry's responses to questions following this career and

business compass are not listed in order to honor his privacy. Thank you, Larry, for sharing your career and business compass competencies with the readers of this book.

> **Do People Really Change?**
>
> **Smart Managing**
>
> "The only thing in the world you can change is yourself and that makes all the difference in the world."
>
> —Cher

Start a Binder or Journal

Okay, now you've seen an example. It's your turn. Get to your computer now, or get lots of paper to write on. Better yet, start a binder or journal with your personal responses to these

---

Career and Business Compass: Competency Exercise

Contributed in a workshop by Larry Madison, Grand Rapids, Michigan

My Present Situation: What's Going on and How I Feel about It

I am presently working as an assistant project manager for a high-tech company that manufactures software programs. The truth is that I took this job because they offered it to me and I didn't have the confidence at the time to wait it out and see if someone else would offer me a better, more innovative job in the area I truly wanted to work—as a guidance counselor and therapist. I lacked confidence in myself big time.

I promised myself at the time that I'd only stay here for six months, but I've been here now for two years and I feel myself getting dragged down into a deep and depressing rut. I don't like who I've become or what I do for a living. I'm angry that I lost my passion along the way and that I've settled for less.

Everyone tells me I should stay where I am because of the benefits and pay. The organization is a good one; it is just not for me. I gave up my dream and I don't want to live to regret not following my life's passion.

(continued)

My Dream:

My dream is to become a guidance counselor and therapist for emotionally challenged students, ages 12 to 18. I'd like to design a school program dedicated to building self-esteem for students of all backgrounds and create a system that follows up and measures their ongoing success and progress over a period of 10 years. I would then like to use this study as a basis for pursuing my doctorate in counseling and later become a free agent and design, develop, and sell programs to private and public school systems on a global scale.

What's Holding Me Back?

Presently, I do not possess the qualifications necessary to qualify for this type of work. However, I've proven through this exercise that I do possess the basic competencies that would allow me to be successful in this field, provided I am willing to make a commitment to the appropriate educational training and skill development that will get me the credentials required. I'm willing to make that commitment and effort.

What's My Plan? Where Am I on the Learning Curve in Order to Get There? How Much Time Will It Take?

I would first have to return to school and get a master's degree in marriage and family counseling. I would do this in the evenings and I estimate it will take me approximately 18 months to complete if I pursue my degree online or through an accelerated distance-learning program. I have identified four potential universities and financial aid programs that meet my needs. In the meantime, I will volunteer one weekend a month at my local middle-school, helping to create a self-esteem program for students and assist with developing a measurement tool that the school will be able to use for ongoing improvement and learning purposes.

Feedback to the Facilitator:

Attending Anne Bruce's workshop, *Be Your Own Mentor,* has helped me to reconnect with my real talents and competencies, both soft and hard skill sets. I can see clearly now where all the gaps are and what I've let fall through the cracks in my life. After completing the 10 premium self-mentoring compasses exercise, I feel back on track. I still have a lot of work to do, but overall, I have a stronger sense now of where I am going and why I want to go there! I'm starting my plan of action first thing in the morning. This self-mentoring thing really works!

Here Larry identifies his emotional and soft-skill competencies and his intellectual and hard-skill competencies in order to assess his potential for a major career change.

My Strongest Interests, Talents, and Human Characteristics (Soft Skills)	My Technical Skills, Cognitive Ability, Education, Experience, and Skill Sets (Hard Skills)
Caring for the development of teens Designing personality assessments Influencing young minds Being humorous, enjoying life Counseling and therapy techniques Listening Coaching kids Finding solutions Mediating Heading up projects and completing them Envisioning possibilities for kids Improving the public school system with new and innovative ideas Personality assessment design Working with kids and helping them achieve their greatest potential	Asst. Project mgr. 2 years experience BS degree in engineering and political science Critical thinker Good at implementing strategies Keen understanding of sciences and mathematics and measurement tools Precise in my work Technical writing and creative writing Projecting and meeting deadlines Computer savvy and can design software and implement new systems easily Train others Facilitate the success of others on the job

Applying Competencies

In our global economy and workplace, the word *competency* can have many interpretations. These meanings can sometimes be related to tasks and results, such as making deals, organizing things, crunching the numbers, or retooling work environments. Other times they can describe characteristics or behaviors of the people doing the job, such as a person's awakening spirit, outgoing nature, outrageous sense of humor, artistic talents, or the ability to influence outcomes and effect change.

When we take time to identify our vast array of competencies and talents, we uncover a powerful vocational tool that can provide keys to unlocking greater opportunities and career choices we might make along the way. Listed here are a few ways your own competencies can be used as helpful decision-making and career tools.

Review on a regular basis your competencies and interests as you go along in this program and let them guide you when faced with choices, such as:

1. Rewriting your job description or detailing the vision of a new career opportunity
2. Creating and launching new projects
3. Deciding whether or not to start your own business
4. Choosing a graduate school program that fits your best interests and needs
5. Selecting appropriate training seminars to attend
6. Choosing team members for a project you are heading up
7. Developing a strategic new career plan
8. Deciding to write a book or become a subject matter expert

Add more of your own ideas to the list here:

9. _____
10. _____
11. _____
12. _____

1. Higher Power Compass: Competency Exercise

My present situation as it relates to my personal belief system, or study of world religions in the twenty-first century, etc. What's going on with my higher level of consciousness and my spiritual health, and how do I feel about it all?

My dream and the level to which I would like to rise in this area of my life:

Carl Jung said: "You are a soul, you have a body." My thoughts on this:

What's holding me back?

What's my plan? Where am I on the learning curve in order to get there? How much time will it take? How am I inspired and drawn to a higher force?

Identify and list in the boxes here your emotional and soft-skill competencies as they relate to your faith and your intellectual and hard-skill competencies in order to assess your potential for change in this area

My Strongest Interests, Talents, and Human Characteristics (Soft Skills)	My Technical Skills, Cognitive Ability, Education, Experience, and Skill Sets (Hard Skills)

questions and begin designing an action plan that you can take off the shelf, review, and implement. Remember, you're the author of your life story, so start writing!

Questions to Answer for #1

- Do you cultivate people in your life who feed your soul? How do you do this? Who are they?
- Do you feel capable of connecting with your spirit without disconnecting from your brain? Are you someone who follows blindly or investigates your inner truth until you get the answers?
- In your life, how do your intellect and spirit converge? What does that convergence look like?
- Do you get opposition on how you worship or what you believe in from family and friends? Do you remain true to yourself, or do you eventually give in to conventional thinking?
- How do you incorporate your connection to a higher power or consciousness when mentoring yourself? Do you follow a daily program for accomplishing this?
- Are you searching for something that is intangible or that you cannot explain? What can you do to find these answers and investigate various possibilities? Who can you talk with? What unconventional, or even irreverent, questions might you pose?
- How does your faith provide you with a platform for strength and hope?
- Do you consider yourself multisensory? Are you intuitive? How do you use these traits to mentor yourself forward? Do you see them as tools for strength and higher power, or do you see them as hocus-pocus? Why or why not?
- Is the power of prayer and meditation important to you? How do you use these tools to improve your life?

Universal Life Force That You Can Tap Into

"There is a universal intelligent life force that exists within everyone and everything. It resides within each one of us as a deep wisdom, an inner knowing. We can assess this wonderful source of knowledge and wisdom through our intuition: an inner sense that tells us what feels right and true for us at any given moment."

—Shakti Gawain

- Have you ever fallen away from your faith and then reconnected? Are you in the process of reconnecting to something now? How are you going about it? Is it working for you?

2. Health Compass: Competency Exercise

My present situation. What's going on with my health and how do I feel about it? Here's how I feel when I look in the mirror. I love how I look and feel in my body and when I don't I _____. I have a healthy body-image. I worry about _____ regarding my health. My mental state is _____ and emotionally I'm _____.

My dream for my mind, body, and soul is:

I am capable of creating my own biology regardless of my genetic make-up. Here's what I am doing to make this happen:

What's holding me back?

What's my plan? Where am I on the learning curve in order to get there? How much time will it take?

Identify and list in the boxes here your emotional and soft-skill competencies and your intellectual and hard-skill competencies in order to assess your potential for any physical, mental, or emotional change in this area.

My Strongest Interests, Talents, and Human Characteristics (Soft Skills)	My Technical Skills, Cognitive Ability, Education, Experience, and Skill Sets (Hard Skills)
_____	_____
_____	_____
_____	_____
_____	_____
_____	_____
_____	_____
_____	_____
_____	_____
_____	_____
_____	_____
_____	_____
_____	_____
	_____

Questions to Answer for #2

- Do you take personal accountability for your overall health and well-being? Do you blame your genes or your upbringing for making you less healthy?
- Do you consider yourself part of the medical team that treats you?
- Do you know and understand your anatomy? If not, why not? If so, what advantage have this knowledge and understanding given you for maintaining your health?
- Describe your body image. How happy are you with how you look and feel?

- Would you like to gain or lose weight? Why? Do you love your look? Why not?
- Do you want to look fabulous, fit, and healthy for yourself or for someone else?
- What is your regimen for good health? How can you improve it?
- Have you ever struggled with mental health issues? How have you learned to handle these issues on your own or with assistance from a professional? Do you take medication of any kind? If so, is it working for you? Is it completely necessary? Are you comfortable with using medications and alternative medicines when appropriate?
- Have you ever had to overcome a major illness? How did it change you? How have you used what you learned from this experience in your daily life?
- What do you fear most about your present health condition? How do you confront those fears?
- Have you ever been in denial about your physical, emotional, or mental health?
- Do you believe that body, mind, and soul are one? Do you treat all three with equal respect?

⚠ CAUTION!

We Create Our Own Biology

Did you know that genetics are only 30 percent responsible for how long we live? Behavioral choices and how we take care of ourselves constitute 70 percent. By the time you are 50 years old, your healthy or unhealthy lifestyle accounts for 80 percent of how you age. Stop blaming your Uncle Mike's genes or your Grandma Nelly's genes. It's incumbent upon each of us to make healthy life choices daily.

3. Feeling Groovy Compass: Competency Exercise

My present situation is very groovy, or not very groovy. What's going on and how do I feel about it? When I feel groovy I look and feel like this:

My grooviest dreams for passion, love, and bliss:

What's holding me back from being motivated or having the gumption necessary to get going on things? I want Chutzpah and I want it now! (Chutzpah is a Yiddish term for get up and go.)

What's my plan to get moving? Where am I on the learning curve in order to get there? How much time will it take for me to become intrinsically motivated?

Identify and list in the boxes here your emotional and soft-skill competencies and your intellectual and hard-skill competencies in order to assess your potential for groovy changes in this area.

My Strongest Interests, Talents, and Human Characteristics (Soft Skills)	My Technical Skills, Cognitive Ability, Education, Experience, and Skill Sets (Hard Skills)
_____	
_____	_____
_____	_____
_____	_____
_____	_____
_____	_____
_____	_____
_____	_____
_____	_____
_____	_____
_____	_____

- What could you start doing now that would have you more mentally fit?
- Have you ever struggled with addiction to a substance, food, love, or anything else? How did you handle it? If you didn't handle it, what are your plans now?

Questions to Answer for #3

- Are you great at home but not at work, or vice versa? Why do you think that is?
- What could you do from morning to night, seven days a week, and never get tired of?
- Do you consider yourself a happy person? What criteria do you use to measure this?
- Are you a passionate person? How do you demonstrate your passion?
- Do you think people are born with the likelihood to be happy?
- Is happiness a choice for you?
- How groovy do you think you are? What does that word mean to you? (You don't have to be Austin Powers or born in the '60s to "get it.")
- Do you have Chutzpah? How do you show it?
- How do you follow your bliss? Are you still following it?
- What motivates you to be your best and live your best life? Is it the satisfaction of doing a job well, being part of a team, feeling empowered, earning money, getting a leadership opportunity, being surrounded by people who "walk-the-walk" and set the example of good behavior, or something else?
- Like Stella in the movie *How Stella Lost Her Groove*, have you ever lost your groove? If so, how did you regain it?
- How would you describe your personality? How do you think others would describe your personality?
- Where do you get your energy from? How do you sustain your energy?
- What's your breaking point? Do you get anxious over little

Managerial Resources

For timeless information, tips, and techniques on getting motivated and building morale, check out some of Anne's bestselling books on this subject, available in bookstores everywhere.

For example, take a look at *Motivating Employees* (McGraw-Hill), *Building a High Morale Workplace* (McGraw-Hill), and *How to Motivate Every Employee* (Hardback: Mighty Manager Series, McGraw-Hill).

A Groovy Self-Mentor Who Runs the Coolest Company

Patagonia founder and entrepreneur Yvon Chouinard has been mentoring himself since he was a kid and took his passion for the outdoors (particularly surfing) and built one truly amazing, very green, and extremely profitable company. Patagonia makes and sells environmentally friendly clothes and gear for the outdoors' enthusiast—clothes for rock climbing, skiing, snowboarding, trail running, and surfing, to name just a few. Etched into the front door of this very groovy Ventura, California, company are the famous words of the legendary Sierra Club executive director David Brower: "There is no business to be done on a dead planet." Above the receptionist's desk are posted current surfing reports including wave size, water quality, and other conditions. And when surf's up, the place clears out and almost everyone, including pets, heads to the beach.

---

things? How does that anxiousness hold you back? What do you fear most? How will you confront that fear?

- How do you control yourself and your emotions?

Questions to Answer for #4

- Do you have a checking and savings accounts in your own name, even if you are married? Mentors oversee their own finances.

4. Money Magnet Compass: Competency Exercise

What is my present situation as it pertains to money? What's going on and how do I feel about it? How do I attract money? Why do I never seem to attract money?

My financial dream:

What's holding me back? Why am I not a money magnet yet?

What's my financial plan? Where am I on the learning curve in order to get there? How much time will it take? Who can I get to help me?

Identify and list in the boxes here your emotional and soft-skill competencies and your intellectual and hard-skill competencies in order to assess your money-magnet potential for change in this area.

My Strongest Interests, Talents, and Human Characteristics (Soft Skills)	My Technical Skills, Cognitive Ability, Education, Experience, and Skill Sets (Hard Skills)
_____	
_____	_____
_____	_____
_____	_____
_____	_____
_____	_____
_____	_____
_____	_____
_____	_____
_____	_____

- What are your money secrets? Are those secrets preventing you from living your best life?
- What are your first memories of dealing with money issues? Do you see your behavior in relationship to money being connected to that early time in your life?
- Has money ever been a source of shame or envy for you?
- Have you ever used money as a form of manipulation or power? Has anyone ever used it toward you in these ways?
- Is wealth important to you? If so, how?
- What is your definition of wealth?
- Are you satisfied with your current earnings? If not, what do you want to be making?
- Are you in debt? If so, do you focus only on getting out of debt instead of focusing on drawing more income to pay your bills?
- Have you considered your potential earnings when you are performing your dream job? What can you do to increase your chances to earn income in your dream job?
- Do you live larger than your income? If so, why do you think that is?
- Do you depend on others for their income to subsidize your lifestyle?
- Do you save money? If so, how can you save more? If not, when will you start?
- Do you invest money? If so, when will you invest more? If not, when will you start?
- Do you embrace money matters with joy or with constant dread?
- Do you feel you have to always pay for things for others so that they will like you more? Do you think there is a connection between self-esteem and money?
- Do you define yourself by what you have, or by the job and title you hold? Why is this important to you or not important to you?

Money Matters Emergency Plan of Action

Life happens—death, fires, floods, broken relationships, and other significant events. You probably have an emergency kit in your garage in case the lights go out or if there's a hurricane warning. But do you have a financial emergency kit to help bail you out when the unexpected happens or if you suffer trauma or lose a job? If the lights go out in your marriage, or if you need to start your life over, you may need a back-up plan. Savings is one thing, but having a money plan of action is another. Do you have all your financial papers filed in one place or in a safety deposit box or safe? Consider: What would you do in a crisis? How would you survive? Suppose you were robbed? Those are the questions to answer and think about. And whether you're married or single, drop the "someone will rescue me" fantasy fast. To be your own mentor, you have to plan to rescue your-self first. So get planning now.

5. Humanity Compass: Competency Exercise

My present situation as it relates to my humanity and the humanity of the world. Where do I fit in? What's going on and how do I feel about it?

My dream as it relates to the greatest contribution I can make. The contribution can be large or small. It may include participating in a mission for the church, or donating a kidney to a loved one or friend. What is my contribution?

What's holding me back from making a difference?

What's my plan of action? Where am I on the learning curve in order to get there? How much time will it take?

Identify and list in the boxes here your emotional and soft-skill competencies and your intellectual and hard-skill competencies in order to assess your potential for humanitarian change and contribution in this area.

My Strongest Interests, Talents, and Human Characteristics (Soft Skills)	My Technical Skills, Cognitive Ability, Education, Experience, and Skill Sets (Hard Skills)
_____	_____

Questions to Answer for #5

- Do you believe we are all one humanity?
- Is improving the lives of others important in your life? How important?
  - What is your signature charity or cause? How much more time and money can you give?
  - Are you prejudiced against a certain group of people? How do your feelings about this group affect your giving strength?

Smart Managing

The State of Humanity

"Injustice anywhere is a threat to justice everywhere."
—Dr. Martin Luther King, Jr.

- Do you really see everyone as one, equal in humanity, or do you try to act politically correct in some circumstances?
- Do you stand for something? What is it?

> **What's Your Philosophy?**
>
> "My philosophy is that not only are you responsible for your life, but doing the best at this moment puts you in the best place for the next moment."
>
> —Oprah Winfrey

TRICKS OF THE TRADE

- How important is it to you to be exposed to diverse cultures?
- What have you done lately to make the world a better place?

6. Abundant Living Compass: Competency Exercise

My present situation regarding living an abundant life is:

How do I attract abundance in my life deliberately? Here's what I do. What's going on and how do I feel about it? Why it works. Why I don't allow it to work.

My dreams of abundance will come true because of what I choose to think and believe and how I behave in response to these things:

What's holding me back? My thoughts create energy frequencies that attract things into my life or push them away. We attract to ourselves what we believe we deserve and are worthy of having—no more, no less.

What's my plan? Where am I on the learning curve in order to get there? How much time will it take?

Identify and list in the boxes here your emotional and soft-skill competencies and your intellectual and hard-skill competencies in order to assess your potential for change to greater abundant living in all areas of your life.

My Strongest Interests, Talents, and Human Characteristics (Soft Skills)	My Technical Skills, Cognitive Ability, Education, Experience, and Skill Sets (Hard Skills)

- Are you an animal lover?
- How do you measure success when helping others?

Questions to Answer for #6

- Do you have the courage and conviction required to live a life of abundance rather than self-deprivation?
- Do you draw abundance to you that you believe you deserve in life?
- Will you compromise up by inviting more into your life and by cocreating with something far greater than yourself? How do you "invite" more into your life?
- Will you stop settling for less when you know that you deserve so much more?

- Have you ever let someone make you feel small or insignificant? Take an oath that you will NEVER allow that again!
- Will you make choices that honor your higher purpose? How will you initiate this process?
- Are your choices in alignment with your Platinum Standards set earlier in this book? Provide an example here.
- Do your choices for a better life honor and respect your two most precious resources, time and energy? You tell the world who you are by how you spend your time and

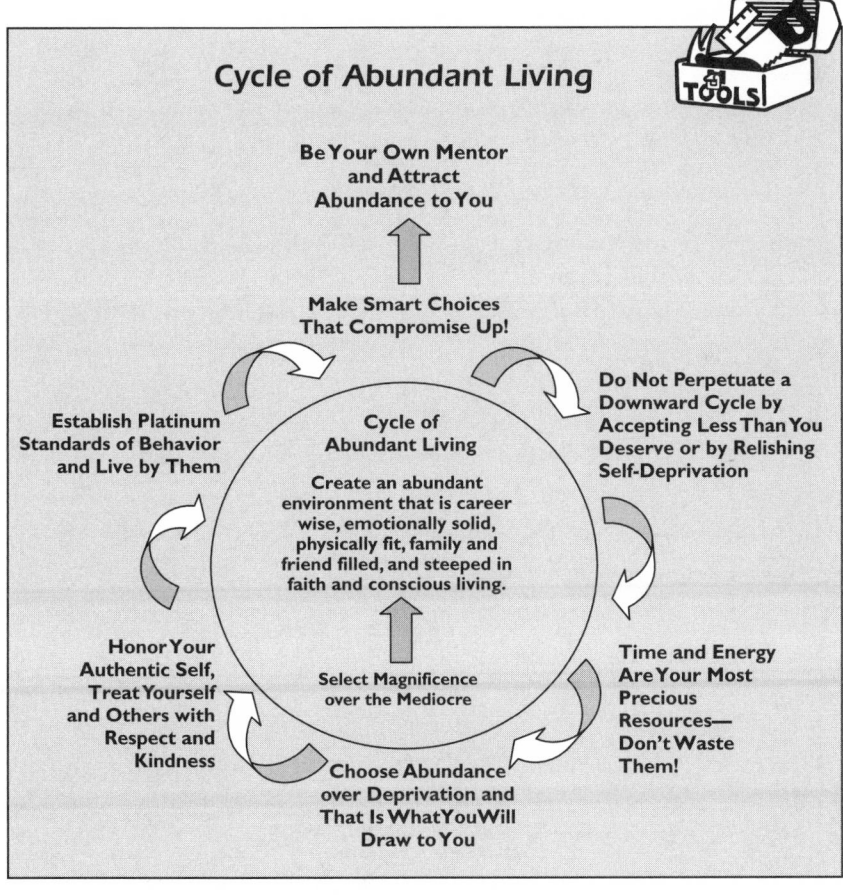

Cycle of Abundant Living

TOOLS

Be Your Own Mentor and Attract Abundance to You

Make Smart Choices That Compromise Up!

Establish Platinum Standards of Behavior and Live by Them

Do Not Perpetuate a Downward Cycle by Accepting Less Than You Deserve or by Relishing Self-Deprivation

Cycle of Abundant Living

Create an abundant environment that is career wise, emotionally solid, physically fit, family and friend filled, and steeped in faith and conscious living.

Honor Your Authentic Self, Treat Yourself and Others with Respect and Kindness

Select Magnificence over the Mediocre

Time and Energy Are Your Most Precious Resources— Don't Waste Them!

Choose Abundance over Deprivation and That Is What You Will Draw to You

7. Intelligences Compass: Competency Exercise

My list of intelligences that I use, can use, or want to practice. Intelligences I never knew I had:

Soft-skill intelligences include qualities such as emotional intelligence, organizational intelligence, choice intelligence, musical intelligence, social intelligence, interpersonal intelligence, and spiritual intelligence. Hard-skill intelligences include attributes such as degrees, technical know-how, training and education, and specific skill sets.

My dream intelligences I'd like to develop over time:

What's holding me back?

What's my plan? Where am I on the learning curve in order to get there? How much time will it take?

Identify and list in the boxes here your emotional and soft-skill competencies and your intellectual and hard-skill competencies in order to assess your potential in this area.

My Strongest Interests, Talents, and Human Characteristics (Soft Skills)	**My Technical Skills, Cognitive Ability, Education, Experience, and Skill Sets (Hard Skills)**
_____	
_____	_____
_____	_____
_____	_____
_____	_____
_____	_____
_____	_____
_____	_____
_____	_____
_____	_____
_____	_____

your resources. How you utilize time and money estab-
lishes your priorities. Have you ever claimed that your
family was your first priority but then spent all your time
at the office?

- Do I accept into my life the best of the best, or do I too
  often accept the best of the worst?
- Do you believe that your talents and competencies are a
  gift which you are responsible to use to the best of your
  ability? How do you use your gifts each day?
- Do you willingly give your respect to others and expect
  the same in return? Or do you expect respect first and
  then give it to others if you deem it appropriate?
- Do you believe you become what you think?
- Do you choose magnificence over mediocrity? Provide an
  example here.

Questions to Answer for #7

- How do your intelli-
  gences play an
  important role in
  your self-
  confidence? How do
  your intelligences
  affect your life
  choices? What has
  held you back in
  the past?

> **Think for Yourself**
>
> "Don't you wish there
> was a knob on the TV to
> turn up the intelligence? There's one
> marked 'Brightness' but it doesn't
> work."
>
> —Gallagher

- How do you apply your many intelligences when planning
  your career success and your personal success?
- How would you describe your attribute bundle? What are
  new and different ways you will implement your talents
  from this point on?
- How has the convergence of all your intelligences peaked
  in your lifetime? Or have they yet to peak?
- How does traditional IQ enhance or detract from other
  intelligences you use?

8. Life Expander Compass: Competency Exercise

My present situation. What am I doing right now to expand my life? I want to make this a habit. I will do the following:

My dream that will expand my life dramatically is:

What's holding me back from expanding my life beyond its current boundaries?

What's my plan? Where am I on the learning curve in order to get there? How much time will it take?

Identify and list in the boxes here your emotional and soft-skill competencies and your intellectual and hard-skill competencies in order to assess your potential for expanding yourself in this area and beyond.

My Strongest Interests, Talents, and Human Characteristics (Soft Skills)	My Technical Skills, Cognitive Ability, Education, Experience, and Skill Sets (Hard Skills)
_____	
_____	_____
_____	_____
_____	_____
_____	_____
_____	_____
_____	_____
_____	_____
_____	_____
_____	_____
_____	_____
_____	_____
_____	

Questions to Answer for #8

- Do you live an expansive life? How so? If not, what's holding you back?
- Taking risks, reading, and travel are the three great life expanders. How do you engage in all of these? Explain. How have any of these areas of life expansion changed your overall perspective of how to live your best life?

> **Authentic Risk Taking**
>
> "Shun the incremental and go for the leap."
>
> —Jack Welch

- Do you hold a passport? What possibilities might travel create for you as your own mentor?
- Do you read? What do you read? How much do you read? How does what you read expand your mind? Could you do better?
- Do you read more than one newspaper? If not, subscribe to one more. Do you read international publications? If not, start doing so now. Your map of the world is a limited perspective. If you are to be your own mentor, you've got to expand your map of the world.
- When was the last time you did something that was outside your comfort zone?
- Complete this sentence: I've always wanted to _____. Now, what's holding you back? Now go do it!
- When did you last take a leap of faith? When do you plan to take your next leap?

Questions to Answer for #9

- Are you trudging through a dead-end career? Have you become zombie-like?
- What is your passion? What can you do all day long, day after day, and never tire of?

9. Career and Business Compass: Competency Exercise

My present situation. Here's what's going on in my career and how I feel about it. I may be considering a free agent lifestyle. Here's what I think:

My dream career or a business opportunity that I'd love to try:

What's holding me back from making a career change or thinking like an entrepreneur? What am I really afraid of?

What's my plan? Where am I on the learning curve in order to get there? How much time will it take? What does my career path look like?

Identify and list in the boxes here your emotional and soft-skill competencies and your intellectual and hard-skill competencies in order to assess your potential for significant change in this area.

My Strongest Interests, Talents, and Human Characteristics (Soft Skills)	My Technical Skills, Cognitive Ability, Education, Experience, and Skill Sets (Hard Skills)
_____	
_____	
_____	_____
_____	_____
_____	_____
_____	_____
_____	_____
_____	_____
_____	_____
_____	_____

- Do you feel buried under layers of obligation in the job you are in now? How can you dig out?
- Where do you see yourself really fitting in if you make a career change?
- What are you not acting on that could make all the difference in your professional success?
- Did you ever give up a dream career because of practical reasons? Do you regret having done so? Do you fantasize about getting back to that point again? Is it realistic that you could? What changes would you have to make to make it happen at this stage of the game?
- Do you let your age hold you back? Or do you think that age is only how many times the Earth revolves around the sun?
- Do you have support and encouragement from family and friends, no matter what you choose to do in life?
- Can you identify the "pay-offs" of why you stay in a dead-end job?
- Are you ready to create your own amazing work experience?
- Where do you fit in regarding free agent globalization? Where would you like to fit in? Are you capable of thinking locally but acting globally? For example, let's say you live in Seattle and want to ship crabmeat to other countries, or you live in Napa and want to ship local wines to Eastern Europe. That's thinking locally but acting globally.

Questions to Answer for #10

- Do you sometimes feel you are in a tug-of-war with everyone over how you should live your life or shape the lives of your children?
- Do you sometimes wonder whether the parenting decisions you're making today are going to have harmful effects down the road?
- Is your family not what it used to be?

Smart Managing

Got a Great New Business Idea?
Learn to Take Criticism Lightly!

Known as the "father of the overnight delivery business," Chairman and CEO Fred Smith of Federal Express said that when he had the desire to get into his own business, he had to learn to take criticism lightly. While attending Yale University, Smith wrote a business paper on a need he had identified for fast and reliable next-day delivery in the age of high technology and computerization in the information age. His professor graded the paper a C, citing that he found the business idea to be quite *improbable*. Smith is quoted as saying, "If you want to be a great leader, find a big parade and run in front of it."

10. The Little Miss Sunshine Phenomenon Compass: Competency Exercise

My present situation as it relates to my family, spouse, kids, and inner circle of friends. What's going on and how do I feel about it? Who's dysfunctional and who cares?

My dream regarding personal relationships and relationships with my colleagues:

What is my dream for my family and my friends?

What's holding me back from having what I want?

What's my plan? Where am I on the learning curve in order to get there? How much time will it take? Do I need counseling? Do others need counseling? How can I help myself and help others? How far would I go? What would I do for family and friends? What wouldn't I do? Would I drive a Volkswagen van across the country to take my daughter to a beauty contest because it meant the world to her?

Identify and list in the boxes here your emotional and soft-skill competencies and your intellectual and hard-skill competencies in order to assess your potential for change within your interpersonal relationships and among friends and colleagues.

My Strongest Interests, Talents, and Human Characteristics (Soft Skills)	My Technical Skills, Cognitive Ability, Education, Experience, and Skill Sets (Hard Skills)

- Do your marriage and family life enhance your self-esteem or tear it down?
- If you could go back and do it all again, would you marry the same person? Would you have children? In surveys, 50 percent of parents resent the sacrifices they have had to make for their families, and one-third regret having had children.
- Can you understand and work around the function of dysfunction in interpersonal circles?
- Do I surround myself with people who respect my beliefs and support my desires and passions unconditionally?

- Are there "energy sucks" in my life? These are folks who suck the energy out of your life with their "high maintenance" requirements of you.
- Are there crazymakers in your personal life or work world? How can you distance yourself? How do you set boundaries?
- Are you good at setting boundaries with family and friends, or do you have the disease to please?
- Can you name three pivotal people in your life who inspire you and make you a better person?
- Who is your best life coach?
- Do you have a life board of directors—people who are experts in areas you can turn to for assistance when you need it?
- Who do you think is a great life coach or mentor? What makes them so?
- If you could take a trip anywhere on earth, where would you go and with whom?

CAUTION!

It's Not Just What You Say, It's Also How You Say It. What Imprint Are You Leaving on Someone You Care About?

To achieve personal happiness, self-mentors understand the importance of eliminating verbal abuse. It's not just what you say and its content that count, it's also the way in which you deliver the message— your tone, voice inflection, body language, and so on. Whether you are speaking to your best friend, your child, your spouse, or whomever else, you are a pivotal person in that person's life at that moment in time. You hold the power to help that person or to shrink them and make them feel small and unworthy. When you yell, criticize, or embarrass someone, even an adult, you are leaving a permanent mark on him or her. Always follow a "constructive" feedback statement with a supportive remark, such as, "I know this may seem unfair right now, but we are a family and we are in this together."

> ### Coping Mechanisms
> Condition yourself now to stop any and all verbal abuse. What signs do you display that say you are losing control? Does your face turn red? Do you get jittery? The first sign can lead to the second sign, so stopping yourself right away is key. Next, choose to not speak at that moment. Cope with how you are feeling before blurting out something you cannot take back, or just leave the room. Leaving the room is an excellent coping mechanism if you cannot reply appropriately. Ask a friend or family member who is good at communicating to coach you. For the long term, get help. Get counseling. Get moving on this right away before you do irreversible damage to family and friends.

- What does family mean to you? How important are your friends?
- Are you loyal? Are you extremely loyal? Are you fanatically loyal?

The Million-Dollar Question: Why Am I Doing This, Anyway?

As we grow older and gain more wisdom, we become more and more comfortable in our own skin. Instead of saying, "Hey, world, look at me, whaddayathink?" we tend to pause and say, "Why am I doing this, anyway?"

It bears repeating. You are the sole navigator of your life. You're the captain, so let go of those unrealistic expectations you've placed on yourself and the need to please everyone but yourself. At the ripe old age of 92, a famous socialite by the name of Brooke Astor said, "When I was forty, I used to wonder what people thought of me. Now I wonder what I think of them." If we all thought this way before we turned 92, we would waste far less time worrying about what everyone else is thinking of us.

You are now completing the first part of this book. I hope that it has set a firm foundation for you to move forward with the rest of this program and

Know Yourself

"Find out who you are and do it on purpose."

—Dolly Parton

that it has triggered your senses, your curiosity, your creativity, and your desire to be all that you can be. From the magnet I keep on my refrigerator and the quote I often use to conclude many of my seminars, I share with you these powerful words by Ralph Waldo Emerson: "Make the most of yourself, for that is all there is of you." So true, Mr. Emerson, so true.

Manager's Checklist for Chapter 2

- ❏ You can't be anything you *want* or *wish* to be, but you *can* become all that you are truly capable of based on your core competencies, passion, talent, and ability to learn.
- ❏ Accepting that something is not right for you is a gift.
- ❏ To be your own mentor you must nurture your nature.
- ❏ Mompreneurs are a growing force in the microbusiness industry.
- ❏ We all have an inner guidance system; we've just neglected to activate it.
- ❏ Self-mentoring is not about having all the answers; it's about asking smart questions.
- ❏ Our competencies are divided into two areas: emotional and human capabilities, or soft-skill competencies, and intellectual and practical talents, or hard-skill competencies.
- ❏ A collection of all our competencies is referred to as an "attribute bundle."
- ❏ Examining the 10 premium self-mentoring compasses is an important step in becoming your own mentor.
- ❏ Ask yourself, "Why am I doing this, anyway?"

So Long, Organizational Worker—Hello, Entrepreneurial Thinker!

When people mentor themselves, they think for themselves. You can't successfully do one without implementing the other. As Maya Angelou says, "It's time for thinking people to start thinking." What exactly does this mean? Well, somewhere along the organizational time line of career advancement, employees, and even some of their managers and supervisors, stop thinking for themselves and instead start waiting to be told what to do and when to do it. We know that when this happens, workers don't do their best work and they are not motivated to act in the best interest of the organization. The question then becomes, "What's in it for me?"

Entrepreneurial thinkers in the organization are not yesterday's traditional employee or manager. Therefore, say so long to the organizational worker as you have come to know him or her. If you really want people to do their best work, you've got to let them feel and experience ownership in the organization. That's what self-mentoring is all about. You've got to think for yourself and you've got to encourage others to do the same.

Say hello to entrepreneurial thinking, even if you work for somebody else.

Make Employees Feel like Partners and Family

Effective managers and supervisors make every employee feel like a business partner. When employees feel ownership of something, they look out for it as if it were their own. It's the same mentality that goes along with why people don't wash rental cars before turning them in at Hertz or Alamo. Why? There's no feeling of ownership. It's also why you don't change the towels in or clean a public restroom. It's not yours.

Entrepreneurial Thinking Is an Action Attitude

A person's entrepreneurial mindset goes beyond profit sharing and stock options. It's an action attitude that eventually gets translated into company profits. You can see this happening in great organizations worldwide, such as GE, Google, Marriott, Patagonia, Southwest Airlines, Apple, Target, Nordstrom, Starbucks, Microsoft, Container Store, Goldman Sachs, and American Express, to name a few.

Entrepreneurial Attitude   Sure, the term can be used to characterize a person who acts too independently, perhaps even as a maverick. It's intended here to convey a sense of feeling joint ownership and caring about the business. An entrepreneurial attitude is about thinking for yourself, like an owner would.

At companies like these and at hundreds of smaller organizations, people take pride in what they do and help make the organization money—lots of it—because they are treated like partners and not like hired help. They use attitude as an action technique to move things forward and grow the organization and its people.

As a manager in today's workplace, you've got to show folks how to think for themselves.

Three Steps to Mentoring People to Think like Entrepreneurs

Step 1: Show 'Em How the Organization Makes Money and Loses Money

As a manager or supervisor, you already know how the organization operates and manages its finances. But you might not realize what it's like to do a job without knowing how every person impacts the bottom line.

When people understand how the organization operates and how it generates profits and pays its overhead and expenses, they become more inclined to think like an owner and help make a difference. So what can you do as a manager to help others understand how the business operates and makes money?

For starters, you can show people how to read your organization's annual report and other important and strategic documents. Many of your workers might not even know what an annual report is all about, what operating philosophies mean, or how to interpret certain aspects of various financial goals. There's no need to overdo it; just take some time to show everyone their individual impact on the bottom line, in terms of costs and income generated. When you do this, you help people to think like entrepreneurs and not just like hired help. By doing this, you tell your employees that each person makes a difference.

Mentoring Open-Book Management Techniques

Over the past decade, open-book management has become a popular approach among managers. Open-book management

The Powerful Impact of One Employee on an Organization

Demonstrate for employees how the impact of their attitudes and actions can greatly affect the organization in dollars and cents. Here's an example.

A customer service agent—let's call her Sally—for a small commuter airline in Cape Cod, Massachusetts, isn't very motivated to do her job because she simply doesn't see the big picture of how exactly her actions impact the company financially. She doesn't "get it" when it comes to how her individual involvement and effort impact the organization's bottom line, or its long-term success, or its failure, for that matter.

Here's the scenario: A flight arrives late from Nantucket to Cape Cod and a passenger's bag must be transferred to a connector flight within minutes. The customer service rep just doesn't feel like hustling the bag over to the ramp's baggage handler. She thinks, "What's in it for me, anyway? No big deal. It can go out on the next flight. What does it really matter in the long run?" So, she leaves the bag on the ramp until the next connector flight comes in four hours later.

Now the passenger—we'll call him Mr. Thompson—has a very important meeting when he arrives at his destination in Martha's Vineyard from Cape Cod. His bag, which contains all of his important papers, doesn't show up. He knew the connection was tight, but it's a small terminal and his bag should have made it all the way through to his final destination. When he realizes the bag didn't get transferred, he complains to the customer service rep at Martha's Vineyard (who had nothing to do with the transfer), and the rep explains that the bag won't arrive for several more hours and unfortunately not in time for Mr. Thompson's meeting. Oops!

As a result, the upset passenger and frequent flier with this commuter airline shares his dismay with all the other passengers who are standing around and then later he goes even further by telling all of his colleagues at the meeting what happened—they too are frequent fliers of this carrier—and they all agree that without the bag they could lose their biggest account! They all agree not to fly this carrier again.

Okay, back to Sally, the customer service rep for the airline in Cape Cod. What's the bottom-line impact to the company resulting from this one employee and her lack of action attitude and entrepreneurial thinking? Well, for starters, the small carrier lost a valuable frequent flier, because there's another start-up commuter airline, just down the way in Terminal B, that's just dying to get that passenger's business. Plus, the airliner lost all of Mr. Thompson's and his associates' future travel business, as well. This translates to significant loss in revenue, possibly tens of thousands of dollars, especially when this story ripples out even further to friends and family.

On top of that, Sally in Cape Cod unknowingly just created more work for the tiny airline's other employees who now have to make up for her negligence. And that's an expense to the company, not income. Oops again!

Now, multiply this lack of action attitude from one person by the number of incidents that might occur throughout this commuter airline in a given year. We're talking about hundreds of thousands of dollars in lost revenue and added effort and expense to the organization as a whole.

Here's the million-dollar question: do you think that just one customer service representative in Cape Cod, who didn't have an entrepreneurial attitude from the start simply because she did not realize her larger impact on everyone she works with and the bottom line to the airline she works for, could make a difference in the long-term success or failure of this company? You bet she could.

involves sharing the organization's financial data with employees and showing them specifically what they cost the organization and what value they add.

A few good resources for practicing open-book management include Jack Stack and Bo Burlingham's books *The Great Game of Business* (Currency Books) and *A Stake in the Outcome: Building a Culture of Ownership for the Long-term Success of Your Business* (Currency Books). You also can visit their Web site at www.greatgame.com and click on their coaching link to meet the Great Game of Business coaching team and research other support packages and coaching services having to do with the art of open-book management. Or you can gather your own resources and start your own process and train employees how to be their own mentors.

Step 2: Emphasize to Every Employee His or Her Important Role in the Organization so That They Can Begin Mentoring Themselves

How can you help your people to become more aware of their crucial roles and feel more a part of what's happening throughout the organization?

You can start by helping everyone to understand the organization's mission, goals, and strategies. I mean really understand. Don't just depend on what they learned in their new-hire orientation. Go beyond and mentor others to understand why their role is valued and why their contribution is so very important. Be specific. By doing this, you make it easier for others to identify with the overall organization and its reasons for doing certain things the way they do. You'll also eliminate the questions employees asked themselves, like "Why does this organization do things this way?" "Does what I do really matter in the big scheme of things?" "Do I really make a difference here, and does anyone really care?"

Mentor yourself and others by providing books, articles, and Web sites about your industry, its competition, and the latest in trends. Provide a historical perspective that will help create cultural pride among workers. Disney is known for this approach and instilling pride in every employee through a better understanding of the Disney story and its founder Walt Disney.

When Entrepreneurial Thinking Shifts Us Upward

You don't have to make everyone a manager or supervisor, but you can help everyone to think outside the cubicle or work station, or even outside the walls of their department, and begin to realize just how they fit in and the difference they make. When this paradigm shift happens, entrepreneurial thinking is born. Remember, in the Introduction to this book, I set up the importance of self-transformation as it relates to paradigm shifting upward. This is one example of when this shift takes place.

> ### Brainstorm
> This term has been used so often and in so many ways that it deserves a few words of explanation. First of all, a brainstorm does not mean brain drizzle. It means storming, like the word implies, with bolts of creativity and electrical energy! The principle of brainstorming is to use the creative ideas of each employee to create an environment where new and different ideas and suggestions are appreciated and encouraged with gusto, minus any worries regarding their practicality or who gets credit for the ideas that are used.

When you mentor employees to see where they fit into the bigger picture, everyone shifts upward!

Step 3: Mentor Employees to Think Creatively

This means you've got to mentor yourself and others to not only become entrepreneurial thinkers but also become creative and innovative thinkers. How can you inspire others to think in new ways and encourage them to innovate on the job? Start by setting aside time to brainstorm and investigate everyone's ideas and input.

Set up a seminar, or session, on creative thinking. (Check out my Thunderbolt Thinking seminar on my Web site at: www .annebruce.com.) Need inspiration? Read *A Whack on the Side of the Head* (Warner Business Books) by Roger Von Oech, or order his *Creative Whack Pack* at Amazon.com, or get a copy of *Tinkertoys* (Ten Speed Press, Second Edition) by Michael Michalko to help you and your team get moving.

Mentor Yourself to Brain and Idea Mapping

The following example shows how easy it is to brain map one idea and develop a lively brainstorming session in the process (see Figure 3.1 on page 91).

Mentoring Brain-Mapping Sessions

Smart managers practice brain mapping, and they also mentor brain-mapping sessions with their employees. (*Mind mapping* is another term used to describe this same process.) Brain mapping requires a facilitator and scribe who can write fast and think faster. Get a marking pen and a flipchart or white board. Then have the scribe selected start to draw a brain map with new ideas from the group. This is done with one objective, or goal, in the center of the page or board, usually featured in a circle. Then the scribe draws lines from this center circle that connects to supportive thoughts and connections to these ideas. Basically, it starts to look like a crazy octopus!

People get to throw out to the group their opinions and simply go with the flow. When the group goes with the flow, they focus less time on the ideas themselves and start spinning off practical applications and methods of execution. For example: Let's say the center thought is the company picnic and annual fundraiser. Tentacles are drawn from that main idea outward and point to what must take place to make this idea a reality, such as a location, guest list, sponsors needed, and so on. Then from these ideas subtentacles are drawn to flesh out execution, such as whom to call and by when, team leaders' names, team members' names, raffle prizes, company-logo shirts to be ordered and where to get them, games for the kids, music, food, ideas for themes, and so on. Also included to the right of the brain map is a separate list of what it will actually take to make it all happen. This ties all the ideas together.

There are dozens of books and lots of resources on the subject of idea and brain mapping. Some great resources to check out include *Visual Ideas: Tools for Mapping Your Ideas*, by Nancy Margulies and Christine Valenza (Crown House Publishing) and mind-mapping guru Tony Buzan's books *The Mind Map Book* (Penguin Books) and *Make the Most of Your Mind* (Fireside). Another good one is *Keep Your Brain Alive*, by Lawrence C. Katz, Ph.D., and Manning Rubin (Workman Publishing). Also take a look at *Idea Mapping* by Jamie Nast (Wiley). A more scientific approach is offered in *Mapping the Mind*, by Rita Carter and Christopher D. Frith (Phoenix, New Ed Edition, and University of California Press). For software, visit matchware.com, Buzanworld.com, mindapp.com, TheBrain.com, and Visual-mind.com.

Brain mapping is a powerful mentoring and coaching tool for generating lots of ideas. It can be done alone, or it can include everyone. Either way, it's a great self-mentoring technique you can quickly teach everyone in the organization how to use.

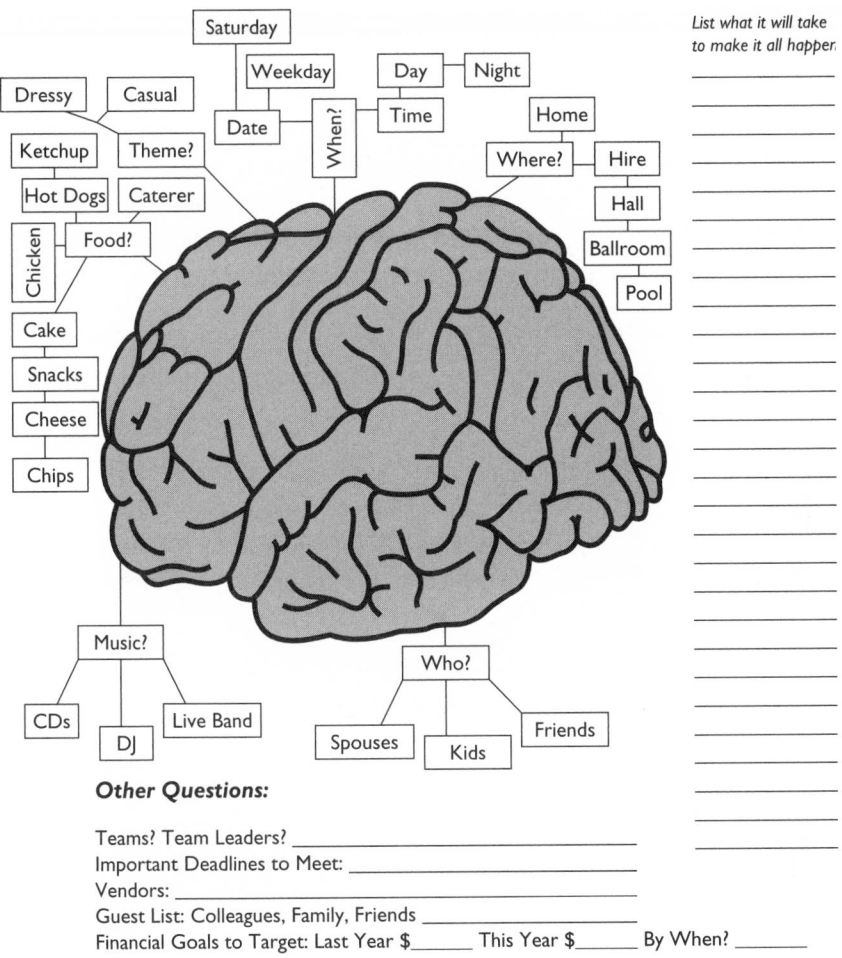

Figure 3.1.   Brain Mapping the Company Picnic Annual Fundraiser

Manager's Checklist for Chapter 3

❑ Dr. Maya Angelou says, "It's time for thinking people to start thinking."

❑ The days of the traditional organizational worker are gone. It's time to welcome the entrepreneurial thinker!

❑ Effective managers and supervisors make every employee feel like a business partner.

❑ Entrepreneurial thinking is an action attitude.

❑ Three steps to mentoring people to think like entrepreneurs are:

1. Show them how the organization makes money and loses money.

2. Emphasize to every employee his or her important role in the organization so that they can begin mentoring themselves.

3. Mentor employees to think creatively.

❑ Use brainstorming and brain mapping as powerful tools for encouraging entrepreneurial thinking.

Part 2

Think for Yourself!
Action Step: Become an Entrepreneurial Thinker—Even If You Work for Someone Else

Do-It-Yourself Life-Coaching Formula for Becoming Your Own Mentor

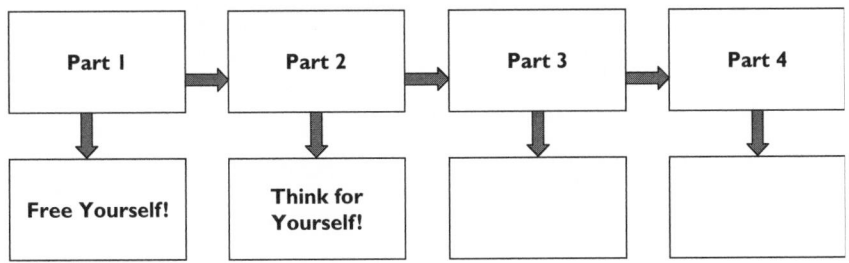

Mentor Intelligent Risk-Taking

Star Managers Mentor Intelligent Risk-Taking and So Do Movie Stars

Risk has long been considered a four-letter word for success. What this boils down to is mentoring new ways to improve the organization and turbo charge the environment for more creative thinking and risk-taking.

Even some movie stars admit to taking chances to get where they are now. Steve Martin is an actor, writer, producer, banjo player, and one wild and crazy guy. In an interview with the *Toronto Sun* newspaper, Martin said that success in life is all about calculating the odds and the risks involved. "I've always been fixated on creating a body of work. That's why I do a lot of movies. Movies are very hard to make and if you do three of them, the odds are that you might only have one that turns out any good. If you do thirty, you may get six that are good."

The point that Martin makes is a good one. Self-mentoring to become great actors or great managers boils down to setting the stage for our greatest chances at success. We choose our

CAUTION!

Watch Out for Foolish Risks

What's the difference between taking intelligent or good risks in business and taking foolish and unreasonable risks? Let's use the lottery as an example.

Would you risk $5,000 or $10,000 from your retirement or savings account on a lottery ticket if the odds were 3 to 1? How about 50 to 1? Or what about 100,000 to 1? At what point does taking the risk go from a reasonable chance at winning to a crazy chance at losing it all? What if the amount you could lose was only $1, or $5, and not such a large sum? Would that make a difference given the odds? Sure it would. Keep these easy-to-grasp examples in mind when you are mentoring yourself and others on taking risks. Sometimes people are unclear about what's good and what's not so good when it comes to risk taking. You'll need to provide specific examples so that everyone understands the difference.

battles and we take giant leaps when we know we've got a good shot at making it to the other side. The fuel to make this a reality is the faith we have in ourselves and the energy and action attitude we possess to keep moving forward.

You're Sure to Miss 100 Percent of the Shots You *Don't* Take

Retired superstar hockey player Wayne Gretzky once said, "You miss 100 percent of the shots you don't take." You may want to consider posting this on a wall at work. It was this risk-taking attitude that earned Gretzky the nickname "The Great One." Remind your employees that, yes, Gretzky has won lots of awards for scoring goals, but he's won just as many for his assists. That's the point. He always helped his teammates to score, too! We can mentor ourselves to greatness, but then it's incumbent upon us to mentor others to greatness as well.

Everyone Makes Mistakes and That's a Good Thing!

Our mistakes provide the best schooling we can learn from. It's from our mistakes that we learn to do things better and correctly. Everyone makes mistakes, and good managers and mentors know that. They also know that developing a risk-taking mentality is a part of helping themselves and others develop an entrepreneurial spirit and approach to better and stronger productivity and performance. Refer back to the Introduction in this book where I point out the importance of being afraid to do something and then overcoming that fear by taking the actions necessary to keep moving forward. Intelligent risk-taking moves us forward in much the same way.

Innovate or Stagnate

Never stop encouraging, supporting, or rewarding intelligent risk-taking in the organization. After all, the only way to sharpen our skills is to try new things and not be afraid to take calculated risks when called for. It's part of the overall innovation process of self-mentoring and mentoring others. The mantra is, "Innovate or stagnate."

Here are seven tips for building a risk-taking culture and leap-of-faith mentality:

1. Allow yourself and others the latitude to make decisions and take risks when called for.
2. Treat mistakes as human. Refer to mistakes as "teachable moments" from which everyone learns something valuable.
3. Expect that setbacks and mistakes are going to be a part of risk taking.
4. Demonstrate to employees the difference between healthy risk taking and foolish chances.
5. If things don't work out the way you plan, ask, "What can be learned from this situation?" "How can this be done better next time?" Don't whine.
6. Be the example. If you hesitate to take risks, why should your employees take them, or why should your kids?

7. Don't be afraid to falter, or it will look like you are always playing it safe.

Are People Getting Mixed Messages about Risk Taking?

We all know that in any organization there are channels and chains of command, assigned responsibilities, and managers who are paid to take risks. Maybe you've been affected by mixed messages from leadership. Maybe your workers have been negatively affected by the same mixed messages: *We want you to feel empowered and take chances—just don't screw up, or you're fired!* Maybe the organization claims to encourage risk taking, but then when things go wrong, they severely discipline the risk taker for trying. Some organizations are so dysfunctional that even when an employee succeeds at something risky, that employee still gets chastised for taking the initiative to begin with.

So start by asking yourself, "Why am I not taking more risks in my life?" "What am I afraid of?" "What's holding back my employees from taking risks?" Then do what's necessary to create a more risk-taking environment. Show faith in yourself

An Easy-to-Use Risk-Taking Diagnostic

You can't eliminate risks, but you can evaluate their potential for success up front.

This four-step diagnostic can assist you in determining whether the risk you are about to take is worth taking.

Step 1: Examine all the critical issues of the risk involved.

Step 2: Assess the opportunity that lies ahead against the objective criteria in order to determine the level of return you can expect on taking this risk.

Step 3: Simply ask, "Is the risk worth it?" "What do I have to gain?" "What do I have to lose?"

Step 4: Stand accountable for the end result—good or bad. Will the organization stand behind its people and the end result? If not, what's your back-up plan?

and in others by truly empowering them to try new ways of doing tasks and providing resources they need to get the task done. If you don't have faith in yourself and in your team, you are telling everyone that risk taking really is not welcome. One organization that has unshakable faith in its people is the Ritz-Carlton hotels.

Risk Taking Is Empowerment with a Bow Tie at This World-Class Hotel

A risk-taking mentality, coupled with real empowerment, is the foundation upon which the Ritz-Carlton Hotel employees work each day for world-class status in an extremely competitive and fast-changing industry.

Here, risk taking is encouraged and accountability assumed. Whether it's a bell person, room-service supervisor, front-desk associate, or housekeeper in the penthouse suite, each worker is empowered to take risks and to spend up to $2,000 on the spot to correct any problem for any customer whatsoever. And why not? The prestigious hotel would not have hired a person they didn't believe was capable of using good judgment and common sense at all times—as any entrepreneurial thinker would do. Because of their great communications style and customer care training, very seldom do Ritz-Carlton employees have to spend a nickel to solve a customer's problem. But if it is necessary to do something extreme to maintain the organization's integrity and reputation, each person, not just management, is ready to risk doing so. At the Ritz-Carlton Hotel, every employee is expected to be a self-mentor and to mentor others on staff, too. The synergy from this prevailing attitude is what keeps the Ritz-Carlton employees in the limelight and winning industry award after industry award.

Does your organization put its money where its mouth is by giving risk-taking authority to its people and not micromanaging them? Does your company say, "Go for it! We trust you will take calculated risks and make decisions based on the best

Motivation to Risk

This quote comes from an Emily Dickinson poem.

We never know how high we are
Till we are called to rise;
And then, if we are true to plan,
Our statures touch the skies.

interest of the organization"? Or does your company practice the "Dilbert" cartoon mentality—us versus them—making employees feel small and incompetent? If we help people to be their own mentors, we create a world of greater human potential and success.

Manager's Checklist for Chapter 4

❏ Risk is a four-letter word for success.

❏ Self-mentoring various levels of risk taking is critical to a leader's success.

❏ There is a huge gap between calculated and intelligent risk taking and foolish and irresponsible risk taking. Helping employees to understand the difference is important.

❏ Mistakes are the only real schools from which we learn to do better.

❏ A risk-taking mantra is, "Innovate or stagnate."

❏ Refer to mistakes as "teachable moments."

❏ Before taking risks, always evaluate the potential for success up front.

❏ Determine if you or the organization is sending out mixed messages about employee risk taking and its consequences.

❏ Do not be afraid to falter now and then, or it will look like you are always playing it safe.

❏ Be the example you seek in others.

The Schoolhouse No Longer Rocks

Welcome to Free Agent Education and the Rule to Unschool

Back in Chapter 1 of this book, I wrote about the reasons why the free agent globalization movement does not accept a world full of outdated work customs and social mores that often crumble under the weight of their own ridiculous structure. I also wrote about why more and more people are using life-coaching methods, like this book, to free themselves from the environment of organizational dysfunction. Well, the same is happening in the world of education. And it's important for us all to understand what the revolution of education is doing to this world—in a good way—and why being your own mentor and life coach when it comes to getting a great education is more important than ever.

Self-Directed Learning Is Required if You Are to Be Your Own Mentor and Life Coach

I bet you can feel the shift. It's palpable. Almost like the shifting tectonic plates on the San Andreas fault in California during an earthquake. Compulsory education, as we know it, is giving way rapidly to self-directed learning alternatives, the most expressive of which is home schooling. Parents are strongly leaning in this direction as home schooling worldwide continues to boom. This powerful self-directed learning mode is continuing to grow in popularity into adulthood worldwide. The brick-and-mortar college is on the way out and is fast becoming an institution of the past.

It's time to accept that the traditional education model of the twentieth century is no more. We'll no longer pop kids, or adults, for that matter, like Cornish game hens into the oven until they are cooked to a desired educational temperature and then serve them to society on a platter ready for work in the traditional workplace of yesterday.

Did you know that the number of students who are thirty years old and older now exceeds the number of eighteen-year-old college students in America? That demographic is directly linked to the changing educational model in the United States and many other countries, such as the United Kingdom. As self-mentors, the rule will be to unschool for higher education.

Unschooling Ourselves for Higher Education

The second section of this book is titled "Think for Yourself," and that also means to get ready to unschool yourself for higher, more customized, education. More than ever, adults must become not only their own mentors, but also their own tutors! We are morphing into a world of lifelong learners and self-educators.

Thousands of companies worldwide are now in the online education business. Their revenues are in the billions of dollars, nontraditional teaching methods continue to abound, and the Internet is now the official matchmaker that brings together student, online instructor, and college institution. Access to the Internet and networking opportunities with brilliant colleagues have enlightened the path to adult learning everywhere.

Educating Ourselves in the Twenty-First Century

- Adults will be expected to learn on their own.
- The shelf-life of a degree will be shorter and an emphasis on changing technology and specific skill sets will be the focus.
- Higher education will not respect semesters. People will demand higher education at their own speed of learning. And most will want it fast and now.
- Distance learning, like that provided by the University of Phoenix, will contribute to the accelerated learning process and keep people learning at home and not necessarily in classrooms.
- More and more people will get their degrees over the Internet.
- College campuses will begin to go out of business in greater numbers and the elite colleges will be the last to change, keeping private education expensive and confining.
- Learning groupies will emerge like never before, attending more industry-related conventions and seminars where like-mindedness is in abundance.
- There will be far greater diversity in academic courses offered online.
- Self-mentors will be committing themselves to learning through national and international programs and services, such as spending time in the military, enlisting in missions with their churches, or joining up for a real-world taste of life with organizations like the Peace Corps.

A Look into the Future of a Self-Directed Learner

The future is now. Each of us will be expected to continue the learning process throughout our lives. The responsibility to do so will be yours, not the responsibility of the human resources department in an organization that routinely sends out memos reminding you that your continuing education credits are due to be updated or that it's time to sign up for your six hours of annual communications training. It's all going to fall into your hands and be your responsibility. For those who are not self-mentors or self-directed learners, it's going to be a tough road ahead. For those reading this book, you've read this far, and that makes you an intentional learner and, most likely, a person who will take full advantage of this unique and exciting time and opportunity in quality education.

In the words of rocker Alice Cooper from his song *School's Out*, "School's out for summer. School's out forever."

Couldn't have said it better myself.

A Letter of Recommendation from the Future
(Excerpt from a future letter of recommendation)
To Whom It May Concern:

It is my pleasure to recommend John Bingham for your organization's opportunity in its civil engineering department.

I have always known John to be a self-starter, self-motivator, and, more importantly, a self-learner. John took the Bill Gates approach to his own advanced learning and development. As you know, he left MIT in his second year of studies and began seeking direction and expertise from the best in the industry and without formal guidance. John opted to be self-taught in this area of engineering studies and has taken an aggressive approach to learning in this field for the past 22 months. Yes, John did forgo a formal degree from MIT; however, he's learned civil engineering quite thoroughly and practices its highest standards by doing work and apprenticing for the best in the industry around the globe. (See attached list of John's assignments worldwide.) His depth and breadth of self-directed study and work experience have been nothing short of stellar.

John is a young man who has taken total control of his education, combining formal training, distance learning, and real-world experience to get to where he is today—a respected leader in his field. I am writing this letter to strongly recommend that you give John the opportunity to demonstrate his talent in your successful organization. I am confident you will be glad you did.

Mary Alice Johnson, Ph.D.

Dean of the School of Civil Engineering

American University of Massachusetts and Engineering Studies Institute

Cambridge, Massachusetts

USA

Manager's Checklist for Chapter 5

❏ Compulsory education is giving way to self-directed learning alternatives.

❏ Brick-and-mortar college campuses are going out of business.

❏ The number of students over age 30 now exceeds the number of 18-year-old college students in America.

❏ It's time to start unschooling ourselves for higher education.

❏ There are thousands of companies worldwide that are in the
online education business and generating billions of dollars
in revenue.

❏ The Internet is now the official matchmaker that brings
together student, online instructor, and college institution.

❏ In the future, adults will be expected to learn on their own.

❏ Higher education will not respect semester limitations and
will move at a faster speed. It will be education on demand.

❏ There will be far greater diversity offered through academic
courses online.

❏ College campuses will begin to go out of business in greater
numbers and the elite colleges will be the last to change
their traditional ways of operation. The shelf-life of a formal
degree will be shorter.

Ghosts of Life-Coaching Mentors Past and Present

When I think of ghosts of life-coaching mentors, past and present, I immediately call to mind the literary classic *A Christmas Carol* by Charles Dickens.

Using its story line as an analogy for this chapter, you might say that the main character Ebenezer Scrooge could also be Supervisor Scrooge, or one of thousands of jaded, unhappy, and miserly managers working in Any Town, USA, or any city in the world, for that matter. To be your own mentor requires understanding where you've been, or how you started out, and then examining just how far you have come so that you can truly appreciate what lies ahead in terms of achieving your greatest possibilities and fulfilling hopes for a better tomorrow.

Three Ghostly Visitors We All Could Use

So with some creative license and a slight twist, a manager's version of this story might go something like this: One fateful night while sleeping, Supervisor Scrooge receives three ghostly visitors. They are the terrifying ghosts of mentors past, present, and future. In his dreams and from these ghosts he gets a glimpse of what is to be if he doesn't take the lead and start making new, self-directed life choices. By reflecting upon the advice of mentors past and present and while anticipating the guidance of possible future ghostly mentors, Supervisor Scrooge can measure just how forward-thinking a leader he really is and begin to institute new and better choices in his life.

Like Supervisor Scrooge, what can you learn from your ghosts of mentors past—some who might have been good influences and some maybe not so good—and what can you learn from those who are helping mentor you presently? When you are able to look back and celebrate your mistakes, or the missteps of your actions and those of your mentors, you often find the power to reverse future mistakes, or at least not repeat them but instead learn from them and teach others what to avoid.

By gaining clarity on all you have to be grateful for in the here and now, you can start to appreciate even more the love and goodwill, mercy, and self-redemption of what ghosts of mentors past may have gone through to pave the way for the future that awaits you now.

From this perspective—ghosts of mentors past, present, and future—we gain strength to move forward and eventually mentor ourselves to our higher potential and stop wasting valuable time and energy on what *coulda, woulda,* or *shoulda* been. We can focus on what we are looking for and feel confident when we find it, much like Ebenezer eventually did. But it took a night of heart-stopping ghostly visits to help him

> **Key Term**
>
> **Mentor**   A mentor is someone from whom you learn and grow. It's someone you admire and whose style and approach you want to study. A mentor can be, and often is, a good friend. When we learn to become our own mentors, that ability does not mean that we do not continue to learn and grow from others. We just take more initiative and a stronger, more self-directed role in the learning process.

Historic Mentors and Their Protégés

Mentor-protégé relationships go back thousands of years and are an important part of history. For example, did you know that Socrates was considered a highly valued and important mentor of his time? In fact, Aristotle and Plato were students of Socrates, and their contributions obviously became quite significant to the world, even thousands of years later. Aristotle and Plato became great philosophers, and their works and writings continue to be held as prime examples in philosophy books and courses taught around the globe. The spin-off and impact that mentoring can have on your life can be immeasurable and extraordinary.

see the light. The message here is that focus is power. Only through the power of focus can we answer the two most critical of self-mentoring questions:

Who am I?

What do I want?

These questions are more difficult to answer than might be expected. But when you develop and create your own life board of directors and mentors, asking these questions is the first step in getting to the answers that are best suited just for you.

Appoint Real-Life Mentors and Coaches to Your Life Board of Directors

In my book *Discover True North: A 4-Week Approach to Ignite Your Passion and Activate Your Potential* (McGraw-Hill), I write extensively about the value of creating a life board of directors. I feel this same principle works well here, too, because your life board of directors is actually composed of mentors past and present and even from the future. Your life board of directors includes those you've apprenticed with and learned from and those you'd like to work alongside or learn more about.

> **Life Board of Directors** A life board of directors is made up of mentors who play key roles in influencing your life's journey in a positive and productive way. You may have known these people in the past, or you may know them now, or you may not know them at all, but they still influence you through their teachings, writings, or highly respected work. Each board member represents a different area of your life, such as business, health, spirituality, or family relationships. You may also have more than one mentor for each category.

Think about it. Companies large and small spend a good deal of time and money courting just the right people and inviting those people to become members of their board of directors. Not only is being on the board of directors considered a prestigious position, but it also conjures up the image of people who are at the helm of an organization, steering its course toward greater success and future growth. So doesn't it seem appropriate that you should take the same approach when acting as your own mentor and select a life board of directors that influences you to achieve your greater career and personal success? Also, keep in mind that by selecting a board, you are not restricting yourself to monthly meetings or must-have work sessions. Everything you learn and apply is completely up to you and how you'd like to absorb the information. Everything is conducted in your space and time and at whatever level you choose to adapt the information you are gathering.

Life Board Members Are Mentors Who Help Us Reinvent Ourselves

To be your own mentor, you'll need to have in place and appoint a life board of directors. Go back to Chapter 2, "Designing Your Best Life," and review the 10 premium self-mentoring compasses listed. Now select a mentor for each category whom you will appoint to your life board of directors.

Write down each mentor's name next to each compass. Remember, you don't have to know these people personally, but you do need to be influenced by them. If you know them, that's great too.

Cultivate Mentors Who Support Your Dreams and Fill Your Tank

One of my closest friends, Traci Van, and I have known one another and have worked together for more than 27 years. As long as I've known her, Traci has effectively cultivated mentors who "fill her tank," as she calls it. I recently asked her more about this, and she told me, "The people who make up my life board of directors are those that fill my tank. Their support, guidance, and perspective fill me with new knowledge and confidence, which enables me to achieve more than I could have ever thought possible."

I love the fact that Traci makes the connection between surrounding herself with the best people in her life and her ability to achieve higher levels of learning and accomplishment at the same time. It's that connection that allows us to constantly evolve and keep reinventing our best selves. And when you think about it, it's not a process that is expensive or even time consuming. It's really a mindset and a philosophy above all. And you can do it, too.

The How-To Part of Making It Happen

We manifest both our personal and professional goals when we cultivate life mentors we can learn from by actually meeting with them, reading about them, or studying their strategies and techniques from afar. It's not something that is done for you. You do it yourself, as it says in part of the title of this book, *A Do-It-Yourself-Guide*. Cultivating mentors to sit on your life board of directors is something you can do for yourself, and you can reap tremendous benefits in the process.

For example, let's say you select someone like fitness guru and author Bob Greene as your mentor to represent your health compass area of life. Write his name next to that premium compass topic in Chapter 2. If you have two health and fitness mentors, write them both down. Perhaps you feel that the pastor of your church, from whom you've gained helpful guidance over the years, is suitable to represent your higher power compass when it comes to coaching stronger spiritual development. Write down his or her name. If, in addition, you follow the teachings of others, such as Gandhi or his holiness the Dalai Lama, then add their names, as well. If you're growing a free-agent, high-tech consultancy business, perhaps Microsoft's Bill Gates and Google's cofounder Sergey Brin are good mentors to add to your life board of directors. Need a financial advisor and mentor? What about Suze Orman? Marriage counselor? How about Dr. Robin Smith or someone you've worked with in the past and respect or know from your community? Want to simplify your life? Albert Einstein wrote and taught on this subject extensively. Need to use motivational tips and tools to get moving on new projects? Perhaps a parent, or a great uncle or aunt who's passed away, provides ongoing inspiration. Put them on your board. See how it works? You make the choices. You select the board members, living or dead. It's that easy.

Smart Managing

Questions that will help you to select mentors for your life board of directors are the following:

- Who would make a great industry-specific mentor? Name someone such as a professor, coach, doctor, or teacher.
- Who would be a great financial advisor and mentor?
- Who would make an enthusiastic health and fitness mentor?
- Who do I know who could help me plan a higher educational path?
- With whom do I feel safe? Who can I trust?
- Whom have I relied on in the past for honest advice and guidance?

The key is to only select people who can move you forward on your life journey. Their support of your dreams or their own life examples and overall influence, both personal and professional, will be your primary criteria for selecting who will be appointed.

Even Madonna and Al Gore Reinvent Themselves— What Are You Waiting For?

Once you've selected the best mentors to place on your life board of directors, you will be much better equipped to reinvent yourself. Think about it. When Madonna reinvents herself every few years, she gets dozens of music industry advisers and experts telling her how to go about doing this in the highly competitive music industry, and when she's reinventing herself as a children's book author (quite a departure, I might add, from the Material Girl's original career), she gets literary agents and editors guiding her along to a bestseller, like *The English Roses* (Callaway). And when Nobel Prize–recipient Al Gore went from Vice President of the United States to almost-President to Green advocate and America's leader of environmentalism (does winning an Oscar for his documentary *An Inconvenient Truth* ring a bell?), he, too, was getting ongoing advice, guidance, and support from lots of people who wanted to be in his camp because they shared the same inspiration and goals for the future.

We watch famous athletes, actors, doctors, airline CEOs, and restaurateurs reinvent themselves every day, but they never reinvent themselves without the help and mentoring of the best in the business. Here is where you may be thinking, Well, that's great for Emeril Lagasse or Sir Richard Branson, Magic Johnson or Dr. Phil, but I don't have that kind of clout, money, or contacts. Well, you'll have plenty of self-mentoring clout if you put together a strategic life board of directors and then follow the teachings and examples of the best in the business and

> ### A Life Board of Directors Can Skyrocket Your Success
> Mistake-proof and lessen your chances for failure by accepting that the many opportunities for reinventing yourself successfully will skyrocket when you assemble a life board of directors that is made up of your most desirable mentors and key influencers. It takes only a small amount of time to set up. Do it now.

other subject-matter experts on your own time and at your own pace.

Manager's Checklist for Chapter 6

❑ Examining our ghosts of mentors past, present, and future can be a helpful thing to do.

❑ It's from the ghosts of mentors past, present, and future that we gain strength to move forward and eventually mentor ourselves to our higher potential and stop wasting valuable time and energy on what *coulda, woulda,* or *shoulda* been.

❑ A life board of directors is made up of mentors who play key roles in influencing your life's journey in a positive and productive way.

❑ Two important questions to ask when reinventing yourself include the following:
  1. Who am I?
  2. What do I want?

❑ Mentors on your life board of directors represent different areas of your life, such as business, health, spirituality, and family relationships. You may also have more than one mentor for each category. When you cultivate mentors who support your dreams, you fill your tank.

❏ A smart question to ask is, Whom have I relied on in the past to give me helpful and honest feedback and support?

❏ Another good question is, From whom would I most like to learn in the future?

Part 3

Reinvent Yourself!

Action Step: Manifest Your Career and Personal Life Goals

**Do-It-Yourself Life-Coaching Formula
for Becoming Your Own Mentor**

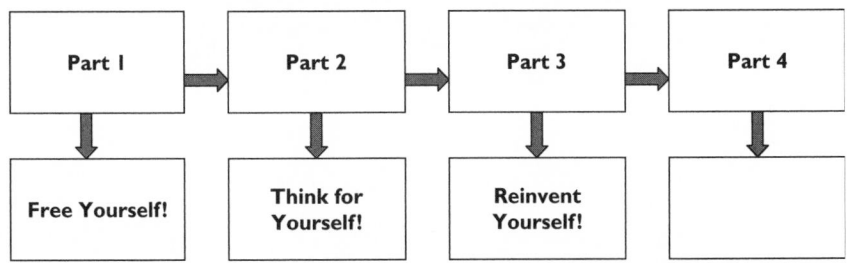

Part 1	Part 2	Part 3	Part 4
Free Yourself!	Think for Yourself!	Reinvent Yourself!	

The Circus That Won't Stop Reinventing Itself

Cirque du Soleil—A Paragon of Innovation

If you want to be your own mentor, then you've got to be creative—a one-of-a-kind manager and leader. You've got to infuse originality into all that you do. The requirement to do all of this is that you innovate. In Chapter 4 the mantra was "Innovate or stagnate." In this chapter the mantra is "Innovate or abdicate." And this holds true no matter where you live and work or what you do for a living. Even if you work in the circus!

Are You Doing Triple Somersaults or Barely Walking the Lowest Balance Beam?

Ever hear of Cirque du Soleil? Chances are good you have, or maybe you've even attended one of their daring stage shows, like *O*, or *Zumanity*, *Ka*, *Mystere*, or one of their signature performances, like the original *Cirque du Soleil*. To see these performers in action begs the questions every manager needs to ask himself or herself: What am I doing to push myself to do triple somersaults and take my talents to a whole new level? Or am I playing it safe walking the lowest balance beam?

Who would ever think that a paragon of creativity and innovation would spring from a circus act? But then, Cirque du Soleil is not your average, run-of-the-mill circus.

Cirque du Soleil reinvents itself and its brand with each new production. Do you reinvent yourself at each new stage of life? When you reinvent yourself, you raise the toughest bar for competitors to overcome and you keep breaking the mold and creating new ones.

Cirque du Soleil: Mini Case Study on a Very Successful Business Model

The Montreal-based performing arts group has reinvented the circus and turned it into an extraordinarily popular and extremely profitable entertainment venue, featuring daring performances that unleash almost unimaginable creativity and that are filled with intense moments and calculated risks like never seen live on stage before.

Welcome to Cirque du Soleil (translation: Circus of the Sun). It all started in a small town near Quebec City, in Canada, back in the early 1980s. That's when a band of colorful characters roamed the streets, striding on stilts, juggling, breathing fire, playing music, and dancing to their heart's content. The entire town was intrigued by the young performers and the man who later became their CEO and founder, Guy Laliberte. The innovative troupe went on to found Le Club des talons hauts, or the High Heels Club, and then in 1982 they organized to take the troupe around the world in lavish style.

Even by the most bizarre standards of the big top, Cirque du Soleil is a one-of-a-kind extravaganza featuring a wide and wild variety of live and daring shows filled with trapeze artists twirling from chandeliers, scuba-trained water performers who weave an aquatic tapestry of surreal theatrical romance, acrobatic angels, tumblers, and unparalleled athletes, all featured in the most opulent costumes and stage operations to create the most breathtaking experiences of a lifetime.

Cirque du Soleil's shows are pulling in audiences that the traditional circus has never seen by shifting the focus from a show geared to kids and families to one focused on adult entertainment, sometimes even R-rated. By doing this, Cirque du Soleil not only reinvented the circus model of business as we know it, but they also reinvented the pricing model that goes along with it. Tickets can go as high as hundreds of dollars apiece, and shows are often sold out more than a year in advance.

What You Can Learn from the Way This Circus Runs

To say that Cirque du Soleil is an impressive high-wire innovative business success is an understatement, and the fact is, most businesses and their managers could learn a thing or two from Cirque du Soleil when it comes to recruiting, hiring, and retaining supremely gifted and talented workers. This circus operation coaxes extraordinary creativity from a global organization with more than 900 artists and more than 3,000 employees brought together from 40 different countries, who speak more than 25 languages—in other words, Cirque du Soleil is its own mini United Nations—complete with on-staff translators. The organization knows how to attract extreme talent, too, with its constant new hire recruitment programs, intense training, and retention efforts. The task of finding a constant supply of talent goes to Cirque du Soleil's casting team—a supreme group of talent in its own right. Casting members, or recruiters, as human resources personnel might call them, show up consistently at the Olympic Games and most world championship competitions to sign the best of the best athletes. Others on the team canvass the globe, searching endlessly for spinners, pole climbers, martial arts specialists, acrobats, and thespians who love to bungee jump. And you thought your company's new-hire roll-out this year was a challenge.

New hires at Cirque du Soleil train at the Montreal head-quarters before being dispatched worldwide to replace artists in existing shows or in new productions. Cirque du Soleil and its leadership and creative teams have introduced a powerhouse brand name to the world that is unsurpassed. Cirque du Soleil has also captured the world's hearts and minds.

In fact, Cirque du Soleil has been named time after time in business surveys as having the most influential and global impact (best practices branding group, the Interbrand Poll) on consumers, over the likes of Disney (yes, you read it right, Disney), McDonald's, Volkswagen, and Microsoft, all while mak-ing in excess of hundreds of millions of dollars in annual revenues—and that's not circus peanuts.

Facts about This Organization

- Eight million people will see a Cirque du Soleil show by the end of the year.
- Sixty million spectators have seen a Cirque du Soleil show so far.
- Cirque du Soleil employs more than 3,000 people worldwide and includes more than 900 performers and artists.
- Cirque du Soleil has not received any grants from the public or pri-vate sector since 1992.
- At the Montreal International Headquarters alone, there are more than 1,600 employees.
- Artists and performers for the troupe represent over 40 nationali-ties and speak 25 different languages.
- Cirque du Soleil is currently presenting more than 14 different shows around the world.
- Major awards include the Emmy, Drama Desk, Bambi, Ace, Germeaux, Gemini, Felix, and Rose d'Or de Montreaux.
- Cirque du Soleil's shareholders reinvest more than 70 percent of their profits back into new shows, initiatives, and research and development every year.

Be Your Own Mentor Exercise

Cirque du Soleil is the perfect example of a successful, highly profitable, global enterprise that must reinvent itself continuously in order to stay in business. Its challenge is to continue to grow at a sustainable pace while offering its creative teams and artists the freedom to dream their wildest dreams and then make them a reality on stage for millions to enjoy. Content providers and managers of Cirque du Soleil accept this challenge willingly and with exceptional motivation and innovative resolve. As a manager and self-mentor, what can you learn from this mini case study about such an extraordinary business model? How can you glean examples and attitudes from the best in the world and use those examples to do triple somersaults in your own career and personal life and not just walk the lowest balance beam because it's safe to do so?

Make notes here and be specific about your commitment to becoming more innovative this year and next:

_____

_____

_____

_____

Describe what you will need to work on and develop over the next 90 days to make this a reality and get things moving forward. What action steps will you take right now?

_____

_____

_____

_____

How will you specifically go about reinventing yourself and applying innovative practices to your personal and professional achievements? How will you measure your growth?

_____

_____

_____

What will be your personal plan of action to make this happen? Write your own mini case study like the one featured here for Cirque du Soleil. How would you present your mini case study to students in business school? What would they learn from your plan of action?

_____

_____

_____

Manager's Checklist for Chapter 7

❏ Innovate or abdicate.

❏ Don't be afraid to reinvent yourself or your business model to achieve greater profits and innovative growth.

❏ Commit to reinvesting some portion of your profits back into your people and your business every year.

❏ Infuse originality into all that you do.

❏ Commit to becoming a one-of-a-kind-manager in a copy-cat world.

❏ Get creative. Glean innovative techniques and tools from world-class organizations outside your own—like the circus!

❏ What comparisons or analogies can be drawn to your own management style when it comes to doing triple somer-saults?

❏ When do you play it safe and walk the lowest balance beam? What keeps you there and not on the high wire?

❏ Describe the most innovative things you've done recently to become your own, stronger, and more creative mentor.

Real-World Reinventors

The action step at the top of Part 3 in this book simply states, Manifest your career and personal life goals. Simple to state, yes, but more difficult to execute in the real world. Therefore, this chapter focuses on real people, with real stories about how they did, indeed, manifest their goals and reinvent themselves through tough times to proud times.

We Reinvent Ourselves Crafting Life's Second Acts

One of the underlying messages of this book is that everyone can reinvent themselves or create a second act in life if they want to badly enough. You can lead the life you want to lead no matter what your age or what you've been through. This second act theory is based, of course, on your belief in yourself and your ability to understand your core competencies and then to activate those competencies with smart questions and action steps.

In Chapter 1, I presented you with ideas on creating portfolio careers. This may be a good time to go back and quickly review that concept, because it works in tandem so well with

Famous People
Who Reinvented Themselves

Ron Howard: From playing Opie on the *Andy Griffith Show* for eight years to appearing in films such as *American Graffiti* and starring in the TV hit *Happy Days,* Ron Howard was always working on reinventing himself to one day become a Hollywood writer and director. At age 23, he cowrote and directed *Grand Theft Auto* and later directed hit movies like *Splash* and *Apollo 13.* In 2002, the reinvention of Ron Howard peaked when he accepted the best director's Oscar for *A Beautiful Mind.*

Roseanne Barr: Surviving a troubled childhood, accentuated by eight months in a mental institution, Roseanne Barr went on to meet and marry a hotel clerk in Georgetown, Colorado. Roseanne had three children, lived in a trailer, and worked as a cocktail waitress. Always sharpening her "act" with customers who would harass her, Roseanne went on to put together a nightclub act and eventually was offered a job at the famous Comedy Store in Los Angeles. This was her big break in going from cocktail waitress to stand up comic to sitcom star. She moved her family to Los Angeles, and the rest is history. Following a string of TV appearances, television execs offered Roseanne her own shown as a "domestic goddess." The show was about the everyday trials and tribulations of a working-class American family. The show is *Roseanne.*

Tom Clancy: Back in the mid-1980s, Tom Clancy was an insurance broker. He worked feverishly to reinvent himself as a bestselling novelist and soon found himself going from writing insurance policies to writing bestselling novels. He bridged the gap when he wrote his first novel called *The Hunt for Red October.* At that time, the book was picked up by a small publishing house that specialized in naval history, but those distribution limitations didn't stop the book from becoming wildly popular among military personnel and eventually getting on the reading list of President Ronald Reagan, who then endorsed the book publicly. Since then, Clancy has authored novel after novel, almost all hitting the bestseller list, with several finding their way to the big screen.

(continued)

> **Michael Jordan:** When Michael Jordan retired at age 30 from basketball, he'd led the Chicago Bulls to three consecutive championships. Jordan redesigned his life soon after as a baseball player but never made it past the minor leagues. He returned to the NBA and the Bulls, and then retired once more. He went on to reinvent himself yet again and became president of basketball operations for the Washington Wizards, but two years later he returned to the court and the game of basketball. The public evolution and what seems like the never-ending reinvention of Michael Jordan has continued into his enormously successful entrepreneurial ventures he enjoys today. Air Jordan is one of the most popular brand names in sportswear and footwear in particular. The products, all made by the Jordan Company, are a very successful part of Nike.

this section of the book. While you're at it, you may want to review Chapter 2, where I discuss how to embrace your reality and understand your core competencies, both emotional and intellectual. It's in Chapter 2 that you started the process to design a do-it-yourself career and personal success life strategy.

In the last part of this book, Part 4, we'll tie together all of these moving pieces with a list of your many intelligences and how you can discover and activate them with new and better life choices.

Right now, I will wrap up Part 2 of this book with a few real-life examples and the people behind them who've reinvented their lives quite successfully, often through difficult times and challenges. Their stories are deep and inspiring, but I've done my best to succinctly share with you the highlights of their inspirational messages.

The Ex-Offender Who Reinvented Himself

As an author and trainer, I conduct hundreds of seminars and workshops. As a workshop facilitator in particular, I find that it's fairly common to have one person in the class or group who stands out. The one participant who is the class superstar takes the course content seriously and uses the materials as intended, tries extra hard, and sets a great example of enthusiastic participation for everyone else. In one recent workshop I conducted in Winston-Salem, North Carolina, I had one such person. His name is Michael Thomas, an ex-offender who once spent time in prison.

I had Michael in two of my programs over a period of a few months, and I knew then that I would write about him in this book as an example of someone who has successfully mentored and reinvented himself and has also helped countless others reinvent their lives.

I didn't know it at the time, but when I first met Michael in class, he was the Vocational Case Manager for Project Re-entry in Winston-Salem, North Carolina. I later learned that the project is designed to give inmates who are nearing release an up close and personal look at the obstacles they will face in gaining sound employment and at the same time give inmates a boost in confidence to faithfully check "yes" in the box on a job application that asks if you've ever been convicted of a felony.

I contacted Michael a few months after he attended my workshops and asked him for his permission to include him and the Project Re-entry program in this book. His response was exactly what I expected—enthusiastic and appreciative to share how he helps others every day to reinvent their lives. Here's what Michael told me.

"Having been incarcerated myself, I don't pull any punches," says Michael. "I like to lead by example and show ex-offenders the successes of prior participants in the program as evidence that they too can be successful at anything they care to pursue. Just about every week, I tell the groups 'inside' that someone who was once sitting next to them is now employed and, or, attending some form of higher educational schooling."

Smart Managing

Ex-offender Re-entry Programs Are a Smart Way to Help People Reinvent Themselves for a Safer, Better Society

Re-entry programs nationwide involve the use of strategic learning and relearning of behaviors and job training to reintegrate offenders back into their communities upon release from incarceration.

Re-entry programming, which often involves a comprehensive case management approach like the one Michael Thomas was involved in, is intended to assist offenders in acquiring the life skills needed to succeed in the community and become law-abiding citizens. A variety of programs are used to assist offenders in the re-entry process, including prerelease programs, drug rehabilitation, vocational training, and work programs.

At Project Re-entry in Winston-Salem, North Carolina, their mission is to improve the reintegration of ex-offenders and reduce criminal justice costs. They also strive to increase public safety through a pre- and postrelease system that coordinates the department of corrections, ex-offenders, community colleges, JobLink Systems, faith-based ministries, employers, community organizations like Goodwill Industries of Northwest North Carolina, and local residents.

Recently, a more focused approach to re-entry has emerged in the form of re-entry courts. Re-entry courts offer the opportunity for more extensive management and treatment of offenders beginning at the sentencing phase. Re-entry courts seek to promote offender accountability while providing treatment and services during the re-entry process.

Don't Talk about It, Be about It!

Michael asks two straightforward, rhetorical questions of offenders: "Do you enjoy being in prison?" and "Are you afraid to try something different?" Regardless of the response, voiced or not, Michael says that he replies, "Don't talk about it, be about it!" He then shares with each person that he earned his degree from the School of Hard Knocks and that they, too, have been educated in that same school but now it's time to graduate and apply what they've learned.

Attitude and Forgiveness Are Strong Reinvention Tools

Michael believes that a change in attitude is critical if one is to succeed and reinvent himself or herself. Next, he says that an ex-offender must forgive oneself in order for society to forgive the ex-offender.

"Throw out the pity party mentality," says Michael. When people believe they are never going to succeed, they invariably and unconsciously sabotage their own efforts. Failure becomes a self-fulfilling prophecy at that stage. "See, I said no one was going to hire me because I'm a convicted felon! Well, you remain unemployed, just as you expected!" Conversely, Michael suggests that the opposite attitude and approach get positive results. And those are exactly the results that Project Re-entry gets, along with Vocational Case Manager Michael Thomas, demonstrating to ex-offenders, and to society, that indeed everyone gets a shot at a second act in life. Go to www .goodwillnwnc.org and type in search term "Project Re-entry," or visit www.nwpcog.org for more information.

The Doctor Is In

There are few people I've come to know both personally and professionally that I hold in higher regard than Dr. Beata Panzegrau, an immigrant from Poland who is an MD of nuclear radiology and now, having completed her fellowship, a board certified radiologist and nuclear medicine specialist at the prestigious and world-renowned Medical University of South Carolina (MUSC) in Charleston.

I met Dr. Panzegrau when she moved in across the street from me four years ago. I had just returned from a speaking engagement in Poland, a trip I thoroughly enjoyed, and so she and I became fast friends and often discussed my memorable visit to Poland and how she began the long journey of her

In Their Own Words from Project Re-entry Participants

Through the program, despair has turned into desire.

T. G., age 41

Before I came to prison, I had everything. Everything but a little sense....
You gave me a "Plan B" for employment. I'm up for work release right
now. Hopefully, I can get a welding job and impress them to the point
where I could keep the job when I get out. I actually thought it would be
impossible to get a job with a felony on my record, but thanks to Project
Re-entry, I not only have hope, but I have the knowledge and attitude it
takes.

R. H., age 30

After being sent to prison I was very depressed and frustrated with
myself that I made such poor decisions that caused me to lose my freedom. My self-esteem was at an all-time low.... One fateful afternoon the
Programs Department announced that they were looking for volunteers
to take part in a class designed to prepare inmates for re-entry into society. I signed up right away and after the first class I knew this program
was going to be my mental and emotional rescue from the residual effects
of incarceration.... I took a good hard look at me! I will use all that I
have learned to make myself a hard-working, law-abiding and honest citi-
zen for the rest of my life.

D. C., age 45

ultimately distinguished and amazing career as a physician
here in America.

To write here all that this woman has endured and accomplished in her young life (she's only in her forties) would be too
difficult in a small book such as this. However, I can give you
the highlights of her persevering ways in a few paragraphs.

A Doctor Starting Over from Scratch

When you ask Beata Panzegrau if becoming a board certified
radiologist and nuclear medicine specialist at one of the
nation's top medical facilities was difficult, she'll tell you yes,
but that it is not as stressful or as difficult as gaining permanent

residency in the United States. I asked, How could that be? Her response was, "You have no control over something like securing residency in another country." But becoming a doctor is something she did indeed have plenty of control over, and her many years of study and commitment to practicing medicine in this country have paid off. It's no secret, either, that in the long journey to get to where she is today, Dr. Panzegrau had to reinvent her professional life.

What I admire so much about Beata is that she is a person who is willing to take a giant step backward in order to take a huge leap forward—a leap based on faith in herself and in her dream. How many people do you know who would go out on such a limb?

Already an accomplished and practicing physician in Poland, Beata and her supportive family, husband Radek Stempniak and their daughter Kasia, arrived in the United States in 1994. However, even with her credentials, the certification process and medical school requirements in the United States were quite different. She'd have to start over, from scratch.

From Physician to RN, to Waitress at the Red Lobster, to Medical School Again

Unable to get into medical school here at that time, Beata was keenly aware of the need for nurses in the United States. Being an immigrant, she could enroll in nursing school as a faster, surer way to get temporary residency in Greenville, South Carolina. And so the already accomplished physician who had been practicing medicine in Poland for years proudly enrolled in nursing school.

It was at Greenville Hospital System where Beata met the program director of surgery, Dr. Spence Taylor. One day out of the blue he said to her, "Beata, you should be doing what you really want." They were the right words spoken at the right time and soon became the first steps in ushering the then-RN working in ICU to apply for and be accepted to the hospital's school

> ### Dr. Panzegrau on How to Mentor Yourself through Tough Times
> - Know what you want.
> - Ask yourself, "What is it going to take to make this happen?" Ask, "What will it cost?" and accept it. Don't whine.
> - Have a strong belief system and core values in place. This gives you peace of mind so that you can sleep at night.
> - Whatever you do, do it well, or don't do it.
> - Say to yourself, "If I fail, what will it look like?" Then have no regrets and go for it, and you can at least say that you tried.

of medicine—all while working at the Red Lobster as a waitress to help make ends meet—sometimes even falling asleep at the dinner table at home after completing a grueling work schedule and surgical internship. "You find yourself just trying to catch your breath," says Beata.

In addition to Dr. Spence Taylor's support while working at Greenville Hospital System, Beata credits Dr. Leonie Gordon and Dr. Kenneth Spicer, both professors of radiology and program directors at MUSC, for their ongoing encouragement and leadership. Beata's perseverance and commitment to reinventing her medical career here in the United States, while pursuing the ultimate goal of citizenship for her and her family, is a life lesson from which all of us can learn.

Dr. Panzegrau and her family were granted permanent residence and citizenship in the United States of America on September 12, 2006. "I believe in choice," says Beata. "I always believed I would be okay."

The Peace Corps Volunteer Who Would Be Texan and Grande Dame of Dining

There aren't many interviews that I do with someone I've known since I was 12. This one's the exception. I selected the people in this chapter to write about because I know each one of them personally, even the celebs featured whom I have met during my work in television. I can vouch for everyone's credibility and authenticity—but none more than Teresa Byrne-Dodge. Just kids when we met, we have remained the closest and best of friends to this day.

Teresa is a seasoned world traveler and former Peace Corps recruit. She's also an award-winning journalist (Columbia journalism grad) reared in the heartland of America—Dodge City, Kansas—and an internationally respected food critic who teaches programs on quirky and intriguing subjects, like the anthropology of food, at Rice University.

A Boundaryless Thinker before It Was Cool

If you go back and take a look at Chapter 1 where I write about boundaryless thinkers and growing organic, portfolio-style careers, well, here's the lady who set the standard on both, and before it was fashionable, or cool, to do so.

When it comes to growing new career and business opportunities, this former Peace Corp volunteer in South Africa, turned newspaper journalist, turned magazine food critic, can attest firsthand to how it's done. Teresa Byrne-Dodge is the epicurean grande dame of the Southwest and is editor and publisher of *My Table* (the only magazine dedicated to dining out and dining well in Houston). Teresa offers her insights on the motivation to keep reinventing herself, especially during hard times.

One such time was her divorce after 25 years of marriage. For a brief period of time, she was even homeless, living out of hotel rooms, raising two children, and trying to keep a fairly young magazine afloat by freelancing articles for whomever she could, whenever she could. She was spinning all the plates and not dropping any of them. What kept her motivated?

From Dark Days to Yellow Roses

"The motivation was, I had no choice," says Byrne-Dodge. "It took me a couple years to convince myself that I would be able to be a success on my own and buy a house and provide for my kids as a single person. I can't say why I was so fearful leading up to the divorce. Fear of the unknown, perhaps? But I got to the point where I had to answer the question: Is this how I want to spend the last 30 years or so of my life? And the answer was no.

"Once I truly committed to that answer, then I just plunged into making a major life change at 50. It was very scary sometimes, but friends and family—even subscribers—were very supportive. I'll never forget one lady who gave me a yellow rose bush with a note about how inspiring she had found my 'journey.' She suggested planting it outside my front door for a lovely sight and positive reminder of what I had been through, so I did," says Byrne-Dodge.

Indispensable and a Joy to Read

My Table is revered as Houston's premiere dining magazine, published by Lazy Wood Press, a small regional publishing

---

When You Don't Know Enough to Be Afraid

Teresa Byrne-Dodge, editor and publisher of *My Table* magazine, describes her mistake-proofing ways and methodical approach to growing her publication from concept to reality.

"I subscribed to restaurant-review newsletters published in other cities, including one published about New York restaurants, and I thought, 'How hard can it be?' I wasn't afraid. I didn't know enough to be afraid."

Teresa says that her magazine definitely grew quite naturally, over time, starting out as a 12-page newsletter printed on a photocopier. No pretty art, no pretty cover, no ads, no newsstand sales, no nothing. She also keeps all expenses on a cash basis, incurring zero debt. She didn't even pursue advertising sales for three years, but the woman she hired to sell ads, on commission, is still with her, as are two more sales reps. *My Table* is approaching 14 years of publication.

house, also owned by Byrne-Dodge. There's no arguing that this magazine of cuisine is a different kind of publication: personal, edgy, and specialized. Each issue offers readers information on local restaurants, chefs, shops, foods, trends, caterers, festivals, and personalities that make the city's lively culinary scene what it is. In fact, *Esquire* magazine's famed restaurant critic John Mariani calls *My Table* "both indispensable and a joy to read."

(People might not know this, but Houstonians, the residents of America's fourth-largest city, dine out more often than the residents of any other major U.S. city. With more than 5,000 restaurants, Houston has enthusiastically supported *MyTable* as its one and only dining magazine.)

In addition to its editor and publisher reinventing herself, the magazine continues to reinvent itself, as well. "We've added the Culinary Awards—sort of the Academy Awards for Houston's restaurant community," says Teresa, and in 1996, *My Table* started sponsoring culinary trips and tastings for readers.

Whether you're a Houstonian or just browsing for haute spots in the city on your next visit, be prepared to find in *My Table* unlimited ethnic options to dining, Creole favorites, where to go to find the best fresh-from-the-Gulf-of-Mexico seafood, Tex Mex star eateries, stats on the history of vodka, and instructions on where to find the most fabulous martini bars in town! Check out their fun Web site at www.my-table.com.

Keeping the Faith under Superhuman Stress

Finally, this award-winning writer and publisher offers these three tips for reinventing oneself in tough times:

1. Accept comfort and help from your family and friends. You don't have to do everything alone.
2. Be sweet to yourself. (Sometimes it will seem like you're the only one who is!) Work out regularly, get a good haircut, have a glass of wine at the end of the day, go to a movie.
3. Remember that you are not your "normal" self during difficult times. You may have less money than you're used to,

be without a home or job, or simply be under superhuman stress. This will pass, and you will be normal again. Or, to resurrect a Sixties slogan, *Keep the faith.*

Finally, here's another person who kept the faith and now reigns as one of the wealthiest people in the United Kingdom— and the world, for that matter.

Reinventing Herself—From Public Assistance Recipient to World-Renowned Author

There was a time when Joanne Kathleen Rowling was desperate to survive. She lived on public assistance, or welfare, and struggled to support herself and her young daughter. She was in dire need of reinventing herself and her talents, and so she set her sights on writing a novel. Perhaps a long shot to some, but a vision Rowling could see clearly in her own mind's eye and write about in every spare moment.

At the age of 25, before reinventing herself, J. K. Rowling moved to Portugal to teach English. This is when she married and had a child. When her marriage dissolved, she moved to Edinburgh, Scotland, to be near her sister. It was at this time that her chance to reinvent her life was finally launched and Rowling sold her first book for around $4,000.

By 1999, J. K. Rowling's first three installments in her *Harry Potter* series had claimed top ranking on the *New York Times* bestseller list, and by 2000, *Harry Potter and the Goblet of Fire* became the fastest-selling book in publishing history.

Rowling went on to eventually sell the screen adaptation of the first book, *Harry Potter and the Sorcerer's Stone*, which opened in a record number of movie theaters in November 2001. This was the biggest sales weekend for any movie opening in history. The movie made nearly $100 million that first weekend. About a month later, Rowling married Dr. Neil Murray.

I'm closing this chapter with J. K. Rowling's story of how she crafted her own life's second act and successfully reinvented herself, her personal life, and her career along the way. Probably one of the greatest lessons we can take from this amazing woman is that most of life's hurdles and barriers are usually self-imposed, and, by the same token, most are surmountable if we have the competency and belief in ourselves to keep our momentum going.

Reinventing yourself is all about movement. And, yes, sometimes that movement can take you a step or two back, but that's okay. It's temporary. Just keep moving at all costs, like J. K. Rowling.

Manager's Checklist for Chapter 8

- ❏ We reinvent ourselves by crafting life's second acts.
- ❏ Anyone can reinvent themselves or create a second act in life if they want it badly enough.
- ❏ The second-act theory is based on believing in yourself and your ability to understand your core competencies and then activating those competencies with smart questions and steps.
- ❏ Don't talk about it, be about it!
- ❏ Attitude and forgiveness are strong reinvention tools.
- ❏ Accept comfort and help from your family and friends. You don't have to do everything alone.
- ❏ Remember, you're not your "normal" self during difficult times.
- ❏ Keep the faith.

Being Your Own Mentor Is like Doing Stand-Up Comedy—Whose Line Is It, Anyway?

Congratulations. You're in the home stretch of completing this four-part program on how to be your own mentor. The final part of this book is all about igniting, or reigniting, what you already know to be true deep within yourself, or what you have learned in this book.

In my seminars and workshops on life coaching and becoming your own mentor, people often ask me how they will know that they have grasped all of the material and are ready to use what they have learned. In other words, what will ignite them to take action, to let go of their dependence on others, and to start the self-mentoring process? My response is this: You will know that you "get it" and that you are ready to take real action when all of the information just "feels right" and is comfortable and you stop assuming that something won't work for you, or that you can't possibly do something well enough. By now you surely must realize what I said at the beginning of this book: *You are the lightning in the bottle.* (You will read more on this in a little bit.)

Igniting Yourself Is All about Adapting Life's Lessons to Suit Your Individual Needs

Remember, all of this should be natural, not forced and phony. So how does this actually happen, you might be thinking? It happens when you adapt the information and processes in this book to your own unique style and personality. That's right—I said adapt the information—it's okay to change things to suit your specific needs.

Nothing's set in stone. I'm not the ruler of all things self-mentoring or life coaching. And if there were such a job, I wouldn't want it. It's not about following my program, or anyone else's, to the letter. It's about you making this program ten times better than it is with your own unique approaches.

Adaptation Lights Your Fire and Fires You Up to Deliver Life's Punch Line!

Being your own mentor is a creative process, and you are the one in charge of setting up the punch line at every turn. I use the metaphor "punch line" to remind you that you are ultimately in charge of how others respond and act toward you by how you select to deliver your messages, just like stand-up comedians Jerry Seinfeld and Ellen DeGeneres. On stage they carefully craft their messages and especially their punch lines.

They know that the audience has made assumptions about the conclusion of their stories, but who cares? As Drew Carey's show is titled, "Whose line is it, anyway?"

You too must bypass your assumptions and be your own person. Don't be constrained by rules of the past. Successful self-mentors get out there on life's stage and get creative. Let

---

TOOLS

A Punch Line as an Effective Tool

A punch line is the last part of a story or piece of information told to someone or a group that impacts the delivery and meaning of the message. It has significance and may not be what the listener is expecting to hear. A punch line often disarms all assumptions that others are making about the information. Humor is a big part of using effective punch lines, but a punch line does not have to be humorous to be effective and to help people to better understand something, or to learn a powerful lesson.

---

other people make assumptions. You don't need to worry about other people's assumptions as long as you stay in control of your audience, be your own mentor, and have those punch lines ready to deliver at all times. Here's what I mean.

The Creative Way a Stand-Up Comic Ignites Laughter

When a comedian tells a joke, the audience is already a step ahead, making assumptions about what is going to happen next in the story. Sound familiar? How many times have people made false assumptions about you or your ability, or your successes? Probably plenty. The thing is, do others assume things about you simply because they just don't know the truth or the full story, or they haven't yet heard your punch line for communicating your entire message? A punch line is an effective life tool, because when used correctly, it can pleasantly surprise others, show what you are capable of delivering, and emphasize how strong your approach can be. Stand-up comics are the best examples of how this is done so effectively.

A Good Punch Line Eliminates Preconceived Notions

A stand-up comedian, like Jerry Seinfeld, for example, is confident and secure in his material and ability to deliver sold-out performances and rave reviews. Seinfeld has therefore set up a creative process for his Broadway shows and all of his acts. He knows that the people in both his live and television audiences are assuming something about the story he's telling and the ending, and so what does Jerry do? He purposely uses what is called a punch line to destroy the audience's perception or assumption, to make them laugh and let go of their preconceived notions about something. Isn't that exactly what today's manager struggles to do all of the time?

A punch line is all thought out ahead of time and is delivered in a way that ignites an audience to laughter. This is the creative process a comedian uses. We all have our own way of igniting ourselves and others to reach certain conclusions or make certain points. Self-mentors go about surprising people with new ideas or encouraging them to expect the unexpected. They know that there's a right time and timing for everything. And just as timing is critical for the stand up comedian, timing is critical for us, in our delivery of what we want to convey to the world. Anticipatory thinking is what helps us to ignite or reignite a person's senses. It's the bridge to activating our many intelligences with better life choices and punch lines (see Figure 9.1 on page 142).

Here Are a Few Examples

- *I can see your point, Mr. Johnson. However, I'm not sure if you know this or not, but I lived in France for three years and speak fluent French. I could fly to Paris and take this project and make it work in no time. I speak the language and know the culture. I'm the person to do this for you and the company.*
- *That's a great point you've made, Sally. You've obviously done this before. I want to suggest just one more approach that might dovetail well with what you are suggesting. Here's how this could work in tandem with where you are headed with this (explanation goes here). What do you think?*

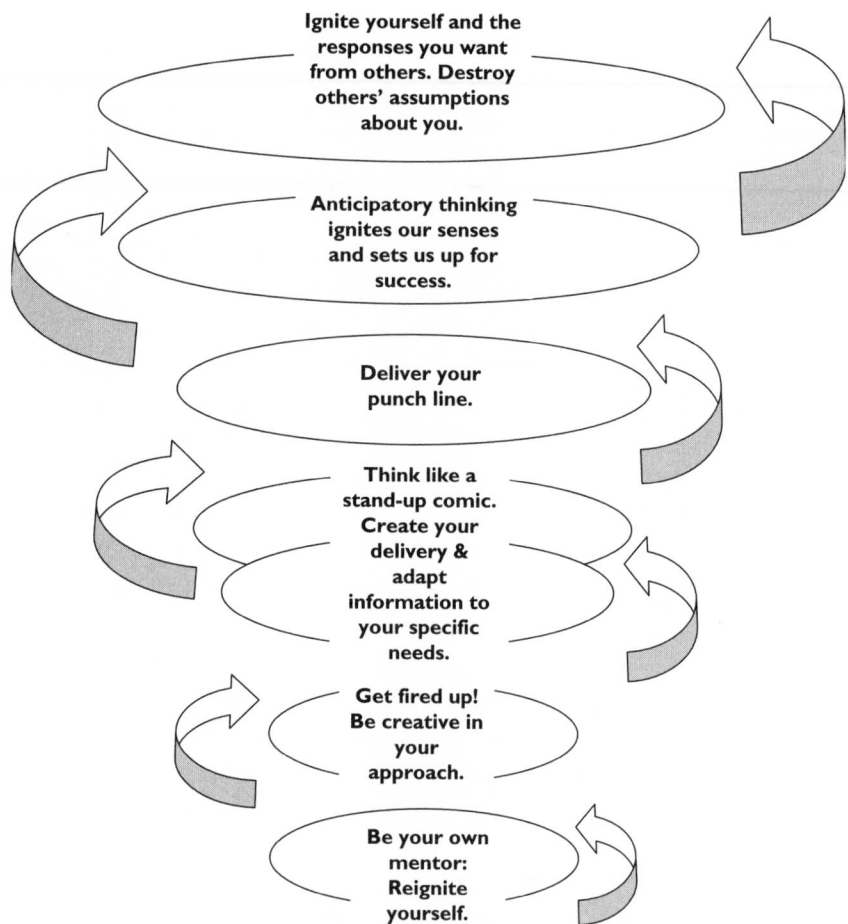

Always Spiral Upward, Never Downward, to Get into Alignment

Figure 9.1.   Using the Stand-up Comic Approach

- *Actually, John, that's not the case at all. I worked in a factory when I lived in Michigan. So I do relate to our workers and what it takes to do this job. I think I can help you to create a new process that will give workers at the plant the flexibility they need and still meet your deadlines.*

- *You might not know this, Dr. Robinson, but I wrote a paper in grad school that was later published on this exact subject. I am confident that we can use this as a tool to promote and market this new approach to clinical trials.*

It's Time to Get into Alignment

Remember way back in the third paragraph of this book how I described the power of taking the whole-person approach to life? I promised you then that all of the parts of this book would align themselves and connect. Here is where they connect.

To be really great at doing your own life coaching and self-mentoring, you've got to be in alignment with not only the four parts of this book, but also with who you are: mentally, emotionally, and soulfully. That's alignment. Think about it. What happens when the tires on your car are not in alignment? Your tires wear out sooner and the overall ride you experience when driving is not as good as it could be. Well, it's the same with humans, too. We must align ourselves so that we can blend together all that we are doing into one smooth ride. Those who learn to take a more holistic and whole-person approach to life rarely have a problem getting into alignment—personally and professionally.

The Human Side of Management Recognizes the Whole Person

Managing and supervising others is about embracing the humanness of people. It's vital that managers recognize the value of people as human beings first and foremost and not look upon their workers as simply revenue producers. When we mentor ourselves or others, we are nurturing nature.

The whole-person approach to training and managing others includes these four human components: head, hands, heart and soulfulness, and feet. Each of these human components represents the human qualities, skills, knowledge, and feelings that organizations and their managers must learn to develop through their mentoring, coaching, and training.

Here is a more detailed explanation of what each human component represents:

Part 1—Head: Your head represents your knowledge about mentoring and life coaching, your unique expertise, intellectual property (i.e., patents, trade secrets, etc.), empowerment, competencies, intelligences, attitude, motivation, character, integrity, and values.

Part 2—Hands: Your hands represent your specific skill sets, the implementation of those skills, follow-through, hands-on-coaching and self-mentoring, customer service, production, and manufacturing of company products.

Part 3—Heart and Soulfulness: Your heart and soulfulness signify your caring ways, emotional depth, ability to love and be loved, feelings, intuition, servant leadership, emotional intelligence, pride, spirit, connection to a higher power, and hope for a better tomorrow.

Part 4—Feet: Your feet firmly represent the foundation upon which you stand as a person, or the foundation upon which your organization and its leadership are built. Your feet also represent a one-of-a-kind culture, history, traditions, company founders, organizational stability, and readiness to move forward and embrace change.

You might say that these four parts of the whole person, working in tandem, are what align us with our personal and professional lives and enable us to be our best. It's a holistic and soulful approach.

For you to be able to inspire and lead others to perform at higher levels, you will first have to plug into your human side, affirm what you feel, and move forward to meet the desires and needs of your

Holistic and Soulful Organization A concept that speaks to the spirit felt within an organization, its deeper meaning and purpose, or inner passion that lives within each person, and the synergy that exists among managers and their staff.

> ## What's Good for the Soul Is Good for How We Mentor Ourselves and Others
> **Smart Managing**
>
> In the book *The Soul at Work* (Simon & Schuster), authors Roger Lewin and Birute Regine write of the powerful ways that managers are learning to respect the soul of the organization, as well as the souls of their workers.
>
> This powerful way of thinking is more human-oriented and breeds greater success and confidence in the workplace by creating an atmosphere of honest relationships and mutual respect. The words of Peter Senge sum it up best: "As we enter the 21st century, it is timely, perhaps even critical, that we recall what humans have understood for a very long time. That working together can indeed be a deep source of life meaning. Anything less is just a job."
>
> The organization with soul respects and treats both internal and external customers as whole persons. Without soul, the organization treats its internal customers, or workers, as mechanical producers of tasks for which they are compensated and treats its external customers as merely necessary interruptions. Managers must work to close the gap between these two distinctly different approaches and align behaviors in the workplace, because the soul of the organization is directly affected by the environmental behaviors that go on around it and vice versa.

employees on all levels—this is what makes the whole-person approach to managing and training both holistic and soulful.

(Note: Depending on your comfort level or your organization's comfort level in using the term *soul*, you also may refer to this concept as meaningful purpose, inner passion, synergy, or greater strength and power.)

Next, we'll take a look at how the choices we make activate our many intelligences.

Manager's Checklist for Chapter 9

❏ Stop assuming that something won't work for you or that you can't possibly do something well enough.

❑ Igniting or reigniting yourself is all about adapting life's lessons to suit your individual needs.

❑ A punch line helps destroy assumptions and preconceived notions others might have of you.

❑ Like timing for the stand-up comic, our timing is everything.

❑ Anticipatory thinking is what helps us to ignite or reignite a person's senses.

❑ What's good for the soul is good for how we mentor ourselves and others.

❑ When we mentor ourselves or others, we are nurturing our nature.

❑ Taking the whole-person approach to life is necessary to being your own mentor.

Part 4

Ignite Yourself!

Action Step: Ignite Your Many Intelligences and Start Applying Them to Your Career—Now!

Do-It-Yourself Life-Coaching Formula for Becoming Your Own Mentor

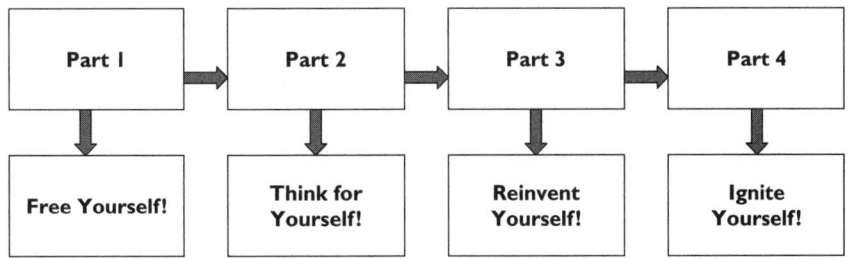

Part 1	Part 2	Part 3	Part 4
Free Yourself!	Think for Yourself!	Reinvent Yourself!	Ignite Yourself!

Why Your Self-Esteem Is Directly Related to Your Intelligence

I like to take a no-nonsense approach to this subject, because it is so important to understand this concept if you are to be your own mentor. The lesson is this: *Your self-esteem is directly related to your intelligence. It is your intelligence in action.* The key to understanding and implementing this lesson is a powerful and effective self-mentoring tool you can use for a lifetime.

Intelligence in Action

In order to be your own mentor in this life, you've got to feel good about yourself, or at least try to gain more confidence and work on your self-image. No one can make you feel good about yourself. Only you can do this. And here's where the process begins:

1. How you perceive yourself impacts every choice, good or bad, that you make. The better you feel about yourself and the stronger your self-esteem, the more likely it is that you will make better choices and vice versa.
2. Choices are not accidents. Each is part of your choice intelligence, or CQ, choice quotient, that activates your mind and intellect.
3. Therefore, it is your self-worth and self-esteem, working in tandem with the choices you make, that become part of your intelligence in action, shaping your opportunity for greater success and happiness.

Self-esteem is intelligence in action, not an accidental happening. Here's the key: When I use the word *intelligence*, I am not simply referring to your IQ. Your IQ is not the only intelligence that you possess. You have many different intelligences. Maybe you've heard of one of the most popular mentions of this, called EQ, or emotional quotient, or emotional intelligence, and SQ, or social quotient, or social intelligence.

Science writer Daniel Goleman points out that self-confident people are often more decisive without being arrogant or defensive, because they stand up for their decisions and choices in life. They voice their views, even when those views may be unpopular, and they'll even go out on a limb, putting themselves in harm's way, for what they believe to be truthful and right. In the Introduction to this book, I talk about self-mentors taking what I call Rosa Parks Initiatives in life. The example of

> **Key Term**
>
> **Emotional and Social Intelligence** In both his books published by Bantam, *Emotional Intelligence* and, most recently, *Social Intelligence*, author Daniel Goleman writes that a person's strong sense of self-worth and ability to relate to others are critical competencies and intelligences (emotional and social). With these intelligences, and many more, you are able to make better choices in life and follow a specific course of action, like the action steps in this book to becoming your own mentor.

Ms. Parks that I gave in the Introduction connects strongly to the point I am making here about a person's self-esteem being directly related to that person's intelligence. I explained then that courage is a choice and choice is always related to our self-confidence and many intelligences.

Implementing CQ, or Choice Intelligence

Every choice you are faced with requires you to activate your mind to make that choice. Therefore you are activating your intellect, which allows you to tap into a wide variety of your unique intelligences.

CQ, or choice intelligence, is one of the most powerful connectors of your intelligence to your self-worth, good health, and ultimate happiness. The lack of CQ can actually sabotage intellect and ultimately your self-esteem. When that happens, the path is cleared for anxiety, fear, depression, and other debilitating disorders, some of which or all of which may keep you from discovering your greater talents and abilities in this life.

In my workshops on choice intelligence, I use the following graphic as a handout to demonstrate the CQ process and the cycle of how our self-esteem becomes our intelligence in action as a result. I think the graphic helps create a picture in your mind that is easy to understand and follow as you study this concept (see Figure 10.1 on page 152).

When you understand this process, you experience what some may call an "Aha" moment. All of a sudden you begin to see the power in the choices that you make.

You Are Where You Are Because of the Choices That You Make

With the exception of very small children and someone with physiological and mental challenges, people are where they are because of the choices that they make in life. If you choose to eat one more piece of cake, you choose to deal with possibly gaining back the weight you just lost. If you choose to drink more alcohol than you can handle, you choose to possibly

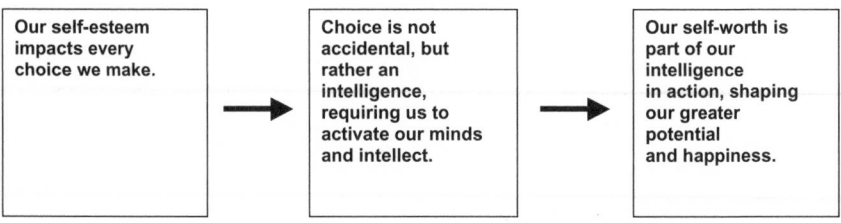

The Cycle of How Our Self-Esteem
Transforms Us and Becomes Our Intelligence in Action

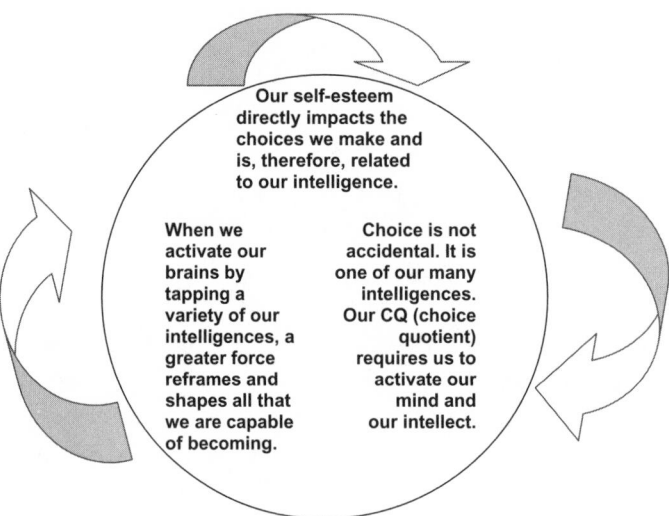

Figure 10.1.   CQ (Choice Quotient) Process for Activating
Potential

behave badly and suffer the consequences. If you choose to
stay in a physically abusive relationship, you very well may be
selecting a death sentence at some point in time. If you want to
see different results in your life, begin by making new choices.

Choices Based on Self-Perception

Start by tapping into all forms of your intelligence—intellectual,
choice, bodily, social, organizational, cultural, decision-making,

---

If You Don't Believe You Are Accountable for Your Life, You Are Mistaken

We all create the ultimate results that our lives produce. In other words, each of us is accountable for the way our life shapes up. Whether things are good or bad, successful or not, it's your life and you own it and all of the results that you are accountable for producing. This may not be what you want to hear, but it is the truth. Therefore, be cautious. Don't fall into the "martyr trap." The martyr trap is a way of thinking that has you saying to yourself, "Life isn't fair. I've been done wrong. I did not create this experience I am having. Poor me." From this point forward, your mantra is, "No whiners, no martyrs." You own your life. Now do something with it. Create something really great. Start making different choices and you'll see different results in a hurry.

---

critical thinking, and so on. Self-mentoring requires that you allow your many intelligences to shape your life choices. Studies show that when we feel good about ourselves we tend to make better life choices, and when we are stuck in a place of low self-confidence we tend to make poor choices that are not in our best interest. Can you think of times when you made either strong or weak choices based on how you were feeling about yourself at the time? Maybe you chose to marry the wrong person, or stay in a toxic relationship. Or perhaps you chose the opposite. Maybe you chose to maintain your dignity and put your integrity and self-worth first, and so you made life choices that took you in a totally different direction, maybe toward graduate school, a new beau, or a geographical move to a location with more opportunity for you and your family. It's always the force behind the choices that you make that gives you the power to feel worthy and to attract greater abundance in life.

You Are Always Negotiating Your Self-Worth

Throughout your lifetime, your self-worth is likely to fluctuate. Yes, there are some times when you are actually smarter than you are at other times. We tap into our different intelligences at various times in our life, and we are always negotiating our sense of self-worth and self-awareness at various stages, as well. This is how we calibrate the 10 premium self-mentoring compasses you learned about in Chapter 2. It's during these fluctuating stages of life that you are making critical choices often based on the way you see yourself. Whether or not those choices are good or bad, they are the choices you are making at that moment in time, like the choice Rosa Parks made on the bus that fateful day in Alabama.

Hundreds of Intelligences to Choose From

If you want to be your own mentor, then know that there are literally hundreds of intelligences to choose from that can help activate your choices. Eight of the most powerful, or the ones you may be most familiar with, are listed in the graphic called Self-Esteem Is Intelligence in Action (see Figure 10.2 on page 156). But in addition to these, you may see yourself in the following intelligences. Just add the word *intelligence* after each word.

- Entrepreneurial
- Cultural
- Musical
- Decision-making
- Critical-thinking
- Communicative
- Empathetic
- Intuitive
- Personable
- Charismatic
- Truthful
- Authentic
- Multisensory
- Intentional
- Soulful

- Sacred
- Global
- Mentoring
- Self-mentoring
- Life-coaching
- Organizational
- Health
- Fitness
- Generous
- Bilingual
- Travel
- Literary
- Risk
- Confidence
- Creative
- Scientific
- Mathematical
- Green
- Earth

What Really Predicts Your Success in Life

Preconceived notions about people and their levels of intelligence are finally being revisited, thanks to scientific researchers like Daniel Goleman and others who study this field of human awareness and behavior and oh, yes, "people smarts." We know now that each of us is smart in different ways that may have little or nothing to do with traditional IQ scores. Our aptitude and our attitude about what makes us smart help us to make smart choices, whether that be in our work, relationships, fitness, or family matters—basically all of the 10 premium self-mentoring compasses found in Chapter 2. This approach has led the world to rethink that being attuned to your own feelings and getting along with others may better predict your success in life than what an IQ test may say about you.

8 Sample Core Intelligences in Action	When Self-Esteem Impacts Intelligence of All Kinds
1. Choice Intelligence	1. Choices only you can make, which activate your mind and self-esteem in tandem, making choices that empower and energize you, choices that contribute to a level of more positive self-awareness.
2. Emotional Intelligence	2. Made up of "soft-skill" competencies, such as integrity, listening, patience, and persistence.
3. Bodily Intelligence	3. Carrying oneself with pride, walking and talking with confidence and greater self-assurance,creating a regal, or charismatic, presence.
4. Spiritual Intelligence	4. To contemplate greater purpose and soulfulness, develop a spiritual framework of beliefs.
5. Social Skills Intelligence	5. Interact with people, build positive relationships, behave wisely, and relate to others.
6. Intrapersonal Intelligence	6. High level of self-actualization and empathy, and can respond to questions, such as, "Who am I?" and "What do I want?"
7. Interpersonal Intelligence	7. Has the ability to understand other people's needs, works cooperatively with others, and is competent at managing relationships and leading teams.
8. Intelligence Quotient (IQ)	8. Ranking or number that denotes a person's intelligence relative to the average.

Figure 10.2.   Self-Esteem Is Intelligence in Action

Reshaping All That You Are Capable of Becoming

By understanding and recognizing the different shapes and appearances of your unique human intelligences and what those intelligences may look like in action, you can better prepare for greater career and personal success as this book promises.

Manager's Checklist for Chapter 10

❏ It's time to rethink how we view people smarts and intelligence in our world.

❏ Self-esteem is directly related to your intelligence.

❏ The word *intelligence* does not just refer to a person's IQ. It can also refer to other areas, such as emotional and social intelligence.

❏ Self-confident people are often more decisive and stand up for their decisions.

❏ CQ is choice quotient, or choice intelligence.

❏ The CQ process and the cycle of our self-esteem become our intelligence in action.

❏ Self-esteem impacts every choice you make.

❏ Choice is not accidental, but rather an intelligence that requires us to activate our minds and intellect.

❏ You are where you are because of the choices that you make.

❏ There are hundreds of intelligences to choose from, including cultural, global, multilingual, decision-making, intuitive, spiritual, scientific, green, and charismatic.

❏ Each of us is smart in different ways that may have little or nothing to do with traditional IQ scores.

Reignite Yourself with the Power of Karma

I am a firm believer in Karma. Karma can ignite and reignite us. If you are to be your own mentor, you'll discover that the way you treat people, the good that you do for others, and the generosity you bestow upon friends, family, and coworkers, minus any expectations of getting something in return, will indeed come back to you. Ever hear the phrase, "What goes around comes around"? That's Karma.

Karma The Hindu and Buddhist philosophy according to which the quality of people's current and future lives is determined by their behavior and treatment of others. The most common term for this philosophy that is used in the Western world is, "What goes around, comes around."

What Are You Putting Out There? Is It Glorious or Is It Toxic?

Ask yourself, "What is it that I am putting out there?" Because whatever it is, it is going to come back to you one way or another. Is what you put out there glorious or toxic? Are you a contributor to or a contaminator of this world?

You are the mirror reflection of what forms around you. If you are a generally positive and helpful person, or a friendly person willing to help others when they need it, you can be sure that you are forming an imprint on the world and leaving mental impressions on those around you. You're creating your own Karma. So when someone needs a person who is proactive, someone who demonstrates a great attitude, you may very well be the person who springs to mind. Conversely, if you are a mean and angry person, someone who is disgruntled all the

---

Minimize the Bad Knowing That Life Is Reciprocal

I'd like to offer a personal observation here. When my daughter, Autumn, went backpacking around the world for one year, at age 26, I thought about her constantly and of course I always wondered, Where is she now? What is she doing? When will I get her next e-mail from perhaps a youth hostel in China or from a monastery in Cambodia, where she is studying with monks? Is she safe and happy taking this extraordinary and rigorous life journey?

What I did not do is worry incessantly. Why? Because I truly believed that my daughter would attract to her the mirror reflection of all the good that she puts out into the world. I've watched her create her own Karma since the day she was born. Does that mean that bad things don't happen to good people? Of course not. Bad things happen in this world all the time. You cannot control the destructive and bad, or harmful, behaviors of others. Nor can you control the laws of nature. If natural forces ripe for creating an earthquake, a hurricane, a tornado, or a tsunami all line up, then natural disasters will occur. But that's not the point.

The point is, you control your own behavior every minute of the day, and for the most part, you will create your own Karma. And no matter the language that is being spoken, the culture of the country, or the struggles and difficulties going on around you at the time, life is reciprocal. You draw to yourself the mirror reflection of who and what you are, what you have created in this life.

time and complains about everything, rarely willing to offer a helping hand (after all, what's in it for you anyway?) or to offer unconditional support to others, don't be surprised if you get skipped over for a wide variety of life's most magnificent opportunities, most of which you'll never even know about to begin with. What imprint will you leave on this earth?

Being Your Own Mentor Requires Good Karma, Because Your Actions Will Come Back Full Circle

Years ago, I had the good fortune to work with some industry greats from my profession—Stephen R. Covey, Ken Blanchard, Dr. Norman Vincent Peale, and Zig Ziglar were a few of them. I particularly liked and followed the works of Zig Ziglar for years, and I never forgot one of his famous sayings: "You can have everything you want in life, if you just help enough other people get everything they want and more." I never forgot that quote and consider it my personal creed to this day. Although in the Christian faith the term *Karma* is not necessarily referred to, the Biblical concept of "What you sow, so shall ye reap" is really the same message of the Hindus and the Buddhists and supports the truest meaning behind Karma. This also reaffirms what many of us have been taught since childhood, often called the Golden Rule—*Do unto others as you would have them do unto you.* These powerful messages apply not only to your personal belief system but to your business Karma as well. Our actions come back full circle. Maybe that means that our most reliable "social security" is how we relate to, socialize with, and work with others.

So do you practice Karma in your personal and business life? I hope so, because you will find that anyone who successfully mentors himself or herself has most likely benefited from the residual impact of good Karma. I have personally found that any time I have committed a random act of kindness or have tried to help others, without expecting anything in return for my efforts, I have received some extremely positive reward down the line, and at times this happened when I least expected it and maybe needed that extra boost.

Good Karma Will Mentor You Forward and Ignite You!

Earlier in this book I explained the power of your inner guidance system and

Another Perspective on Karma

"Everything you done to me is already done to you."
—Quote by the character Celie in *The Color Purple*

the many compasses that exist within you that can guide you on your life path. Well, the law of Karma fits right in with this principle. If you simply point yourself in a positive direction and with good intention, toward your true north, then the power and process of Karma will fall into place naturally and without any effort on your part. The impact and rewards you will reap as you mentor yourself forward will be distinguishable and will change the course of your personal and business life for the better, and quite possibly forever.

We can all learn a positive lesson about good Karma from Patagonia founder Yvon Chouinard. In his fireside presentation to students at the Stanford Graduate School of Business Public Management Program and the school's Woods Institute for the Environment, Chouinard was quoted as saying, "Every time we make a decision to do good, it makes us more money. It's Karma; it's serendipity."

Yvon Chouinard is a man who has always taken the high road. Many of the life choices he's made along the way, regardless of hard times he endured, came from his own inner compass of strong self-reliance and self-confidence.

When we talk about practicing good Karma, we also are talking about making choices. You cannot control everything that is going on around you. If there is great despair being felt from the remnants of a hurricane like Katrina, or if overwhelming hopelessness is the primary energy in an African village impacted by AIDS, you may have no control whatsoever over what has happened. You can, however, always control how you

MISTAKE PROOFING

Are You Practicing Good Personal and Business Karma?
What Might It Cost You if You're Not?

Respond to the following and record your thoughts in writing:

1. Do you consider yourself a generous person? If so, why? If not, why not?

_____

_____

_____

_____

2. Do you deliberately look for ways to make the world a better place? How do you go about doing this? Are you a person who contributes to the greater good of humanity? How so?

_____

_____

_____

_____

3. Knowledge is not power if you are not *doing something* with your knowledge. Break the cycle of hoarding information. Are you afraid someone will steal your ideas, or are you paranoid that someone is getting credit for your suggestions? How can you start changing this behavior, now?

_____

_____

_____

_____

4. When you sense someone is not his or her usual self, do you pick up on the clues and apply empathy and compassion? Have you ever regretted not being proactive in a situation like this? How will you change your approach in the future?

_____

_____

_____

5. Do you make the most of yourself by connecting people with one another and sharing information willingly? Did you know that you become even more powerful when you give your power away? How you can do more of this in your life?

_____

_____

_____

Review your responses to these questions and begin exploring your innermost feelings about how you practice good Karma. Discuss this subject with others and get opinions on how to improve your Karma for greater personal and career success.

choose to respond and behave to any situation at any time. Nobel laureate Elie Wiesel taught us this lesson from his own family's experience during the Holocaust, in his memoir _Night._ Wiesel describes being a 15-year-old boy deported to the concentration camps. He describes the most unspeakable crimes committed against humanity during his years in these camps and then poignantly goes on to describe the test of his human spirit against all odds during these horrific events. In the end, Elie Wiesel's survival came down to how he _chose_ to survive, how he _chose_ to pray even when he questioned God's motives for allowing so much suffering. Elie Wiesel learned to control how he _responded_ to the most desperate and tormenting situations a person could ever imagine, and he, indeed, survived to write about it in his book, which is a deeply moving and important piece of history.

Karma also is about choosing the high road of positive self-esteem. Remember, in the last chapter we discussed how your self-esteem is your intelligence in action. It's also your Karma in action.

Take This Self-Esteem to Good Karma Quiz

Here is a chance to activate your inner guidance system of higher self-esteem and good Karma. Complete the following exercise. Give yourself enough time to respond to the following questions with careful thought.

1. Do your actions or decisions diminish or magnify you as a person? In what ways?

_____

_____

_____

2. How do you carry yourself? Do you resonate a high road or low road presence when you enter a room full of people? Do you walk with confidence and hold your head high, or do you slump and avoid eye contact with others?

_____

_____

_____

3. Do you possess authentic pride in your actions toward others? How do your behaviors magnify your pride and self-confidence?

_____

_____

_____

4. Do you find it easy to speak of your accomplishments when asked about them? (I am not talking about bragging. I am referring to remaining humble but confident enough to discuss your successes when asked specific questions by someone.)

_____

_____

_____

5. Do you take comfort in giving compliments to others and receiving compliments from others? Or do you cringe when someone gives you appropriate praise?

_____

_____

_____

6. Are you genuinely happy for others' good fortune, or do you secretly feel jealous and angry that someone else had something great happen to him or her and you didn't? Do you think to yourself, "This is irritating and I deserve it more than she does?"

_____

_____

_____

7. Are you overly sensitive, or do you laugh at yourself with ease and enjoy the humorous aspects of life?

_____

_____

_____

8. Describe your body language. Do you cross your arms a lot and appear defensive? Or are you open and welcoming to people, making eye contact and smiling at them? Do you use a pleasant tone of voice? What does your voice sound like on your message machine at home or on your cell phone? Is it warm and welcoming to the caller?

_____

_____

_____

9. Do you feel worthy of abundance in your life? Do you feel that you attract abundance, or do you feel that you

sometimes attract negativity and crisis or too much drama?

_____

_____

_____

10. Do you accord yourself generosity and self-respect at all times? If so, explain. If not, why not?

_____

_____

_____

Your responses to the questions in this exercise will help you to quickly detect whether you are traveling on the high road of self-esteem and good Karma or traveling on the low road of self-esteem and bad Karma, perhaps perpetuating a low self-image and perception of yourself. Your responses will clearly indicate which road you travel most. The objective is to establish a pattern of behavior, attitude, and self-worth. Not everyone at every moment is completely one way or the other. If you are not happy with your responses, then it's time to review the program in this book, step by step, and start doing something about it. Knowing all that you have learned in this book up to this point eliminates any excuses for you not to try!

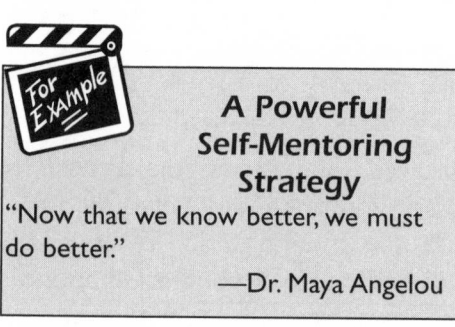

A Powerful Self-Mentoring Strategy

"Now that we know better, we must do better."

—Dr. Maya Angelou

Striking your own blended balance in life and finding your equilibrium are important steps to completing this program and are addressed next in the conclusion to this book.

Manager's Checklist for Chapter 11

❏ How you treat people, the good that you do for others, and the generosity you bestow upon friends, family, and coworkers, minus any expectations of getting something in return, will indeed come back to you.

❏ Karma is a great igniter!

❏ What goes around, comes around.

❏ Practice the Golden Rule: Do unto others as you would have them do unto you.

❏ Ask yourself, What am I putting out there? Is it glorious or is it toxic? Am I a contributor to or a contaminator of this world?

❏ You are the mirror reflection of what forms around you.

❏ Life is reciprocal.

❏ Decide ahead of time the imprint you will leave on this earth.

❏ The most reliable "social security" is how we relate to, socialize, and work with others.

❏ You are the only one who can *choose* how you will respond and behave in any situation you are in at any time.

> "You can have everything you want in life, if you help enough other people get everything they want and more."
>
> —Zig Ziglar

Conclusion

Adapt, Modify, Delete, and Expand

This book was written to help you to make the most of yourself—a do-it-yourself guide to achieving greater career and personal success. One of my favorite quotes that I keep on my refrigerator at home is by Ralph Waldo Emerson. It says, "Make the most of yourself, for that is all there is of you." I treasure these words because they so succinctly call to action our individual responsibility to be all that we are capable of becoming.

There is so much more to you than you could ever imagine. In the words of Dr. Norman Vincent Peale, with whom I had the great pleasure of working, "You are greater than you think you are." I believe this as well. I believe in you, which is why I wrote this book. There comes a time when we all need tools and resources, like this book, to help us along—navigational compasses like the ones you've found here that you can quickly refer to, tips and techniques that will help guide you, a step at a time, toward your dreams and goals.

Mind Expander

"One of the most important things you can bring into this world is the you that you really want to be."

—Robert Fritz, Writer

Make This Program Your Reality

At the start of this book I suggested that this program is just as much about accountability and action as it is about being your own mentor. You've seen that along the way in this program, where I've listed an Action Step at the beginning of each important section. By doing this, I believe I help prepare you, the reader, for greater chances of success. How? The action steps give the chapters "movement" and "motion" and hopefully inspire you to start adapting the information to your specific learning needs. And here is the key to making this life-coaching makeover work for you: *adaptation.*

The Power of Adaptation

When you adapt, modify, delete what's not appropriate for your needs, and expand material from any book to meet your desires and personal objectives, you will gain a practical sense of discovery and growth. You take this Briefcase Book in a series of many and turn it inside out, from a "how to" book to a "what to" book, and that inspires you to keep asking those "activation" questions you practiced in Chapter 3, "Designing Your Best Life," such as *What can I do to put my competencies and talents to their best use? What is stopping me from pursuing my dreams? What am I really afraid of? What should I start doing right now that will create the life experience I long for?*

I assure you that the strategies you've learned in this book have been tested over time in hundreds of my workshops and seminars. So I know they work. But here's the kicker: they work best when you use these following two approaches.

Blend, Don't Balance—Prioritize Time, Don't Manage

If you want to make the most out of the information in this book, then you've got to adapt two approaches to implementing all that you've learned.

Approach #1: Blend your life's activities. Balancing acts are
running families ragged.
Approach #2: Prioritize your time. Time management doesn't
work.

If you adopt these to life lessons, you can make this program work faster and smoother. And here's why.

It's been my experience that after someone completes a
program like this one, that person tries to do a balancing act
by fitting everything he or she has learned into a new
approach to life and work. Next, the person tries to manage
time so that he or she can study the lessons and materials.
These approaches never work and will quickly set you up for
failure.

Beware of Balancing Acts and Time Management—Both Will Run You into the Ground

In the twenty-first century, balancing work and family will
almost always fail. When you try to balance life, you are basically trading off family and work against one another.
Balancing work and home life means that everything revolves
around getting to and from work and day care and back
home again. Everything becomes a mad dash to get from
soccer to the pizza place, take baths, do homework, clean the
house, pay the bills, and try to "live" (and I use the term
loosely) a balanced life. Doing all of this will only do one
thing: leave you wobbling out of balance. Man and woman
were not intended to spin plates from marriage to the grave.
It's not the most effective way to mentor yourself or to live
your life.

So start by finding your equilibrium, that place of comfort
within. That equilibrium is different for everyone. You find equilibrium by *blending* life, not balancing life.

Blending Works. Balancing Doesn't.

Blending, not balancing, life just makes good common sense all the way around. It's consistent with free agent globalization, too, where you are the architect and sculptor of your own life's boundaries and desires rather than jumping to the demands of everyone else's needs. When you blend your life, you practice the whole person approach to living and you simplify an otherwise complex matter. You wake up and realize that blending life is part of a more powerful and broader cultural trend going on around you. Just look and you'll see it in the way people take control of their health. Many people today don't try to balance their health care; instead, they choose to blend traditional medicine with alternative medicines, selecting different and varied forms of treatment and medicines, herbs, or vitamins. Just because you take an antibiotic doesn't mean you can't take vitamin C or Echinacea, too. That's blending.

There are blended families and blended workplaces. In family life we see it with interfaith couples, spawning new religious traditions that incorporate Christmas with Hannuka, Bar Mitzvahs with Confirmations and Baptisms, Ramadan with Kwanzaa. In the workplace we see blending in diversity training and community outreach programs that are growing in leaps and bounds.

Stop Trying to Manage Time

I don't teach time management classes because they simply do not work. There are 24 hours in each day. You cannot manage or change that. What you can do, however, is choose what you will do with that specific block of time each day. That is choice management, not time management. It all comes down to how you prioritize. And adults always will do what is most important to them, no matter what they might say. You might say that time with your family is your greatest priority, but if you are gone six or seven days a week working and never see your family, then it is my guess that work is your greatest priority, not your family.

How can you tell a person's most important priorities in life? Where they spend their time, and how they spend their money. That's it. That tells the story. Take a good look at your calendar. Where are you spending your time these days? And how much time are you spending there? Next, look at your credit card statements and banking accounts. Where are you spending most of your money? Is it on home improvements or wining and dining clients?

The point is this: you cannot manage time, but you can manage relationships and what you do with the time you invest in those relationships.

One Size Fits All, Doesn't

Finding life's mix that works for you is what will work best in the end. The term one size fits all, doesn't. Your size is your size and my size is my size. And that's what fits. High-tech marketing directors in California's Silicon Valley call this "cool fusion." It's the paradigm shift from having to select doing things one way or the other, or blending lots of solutions with lots of choices when life throws you curve balls.

Renew Yourself and Write Your Own Philosophy

Being your own mentor requires times of renewal. This means the renewal of your head, heart, talents, and the willingness to move forward in the face of fear and doubt.

You renew yourself with new thoughts. Your thoughts lead to your feelings, and ultimately lead to your actions. So thoughts are quite important in your ultimate destiny because you truly become the result of all your thoughts.

The final exercise I have for you in this book is to write your own philosophy. It can be a personal philosophy or a business philosophy. It is my belief that when you take time to do this,

TRICKS OF THE TRADE

Cool Fusion with Elegance

Anne Newall is the founder and president of Performax, a life coaching organization located in Charleston, South Carolina. Anne is a teacher, trainer, mentor, and consultant to Fortune 500 companies. She's also a great example of someone who practices "cool fusion" with elegance.

When Anne was diagnosed with breast cancer, she found ways to blend lots of solutions to gain a new lease on life. She's built her business and career on the principles of intentional thought and deliberate success. "Life throws all of us curve balls every single day," says Newall. The difference between those who seem to handle them smoothly and those who stay stuck in drama, or 'bad luck,' is based on the willingness to see how events trigger our responses and grow to something better." Newall stresses that people would be better off if, when they discovered that they were not happy with any areas in their lives, they would just take a look at their own behaviors and history and not focus on just the circumstances that surround them. On her Web site, www.performax.us, Newall states that many give lip service to upfront thought and planning, but few actually practice it.

you answer the questions I presented earlier in this book: Who am I and what do I want?

So take time here to write your philosophy. One might be your business philosophy and another might be your personal life philosophy. Or you may choose to join them together.

My Philosophy by _____ (your name here) _____

_____

_____

_____

_____

_____

_____

_____

Philosophy with Purpose

The reason I have found this exercise to be so powerful, is due to something my goddaughter, Katie McKissick, once wrote on her Web site when she was an undergrad student at USC in Los Angeles. I thought it quite profound that a college student would post a philosophy on her personal Web site. Here's an excerpt from what she wrote:

My teaching philosophy is fairly simple: If your class is boring, so are you. I have always been aware of my teacher's respective styles, and I always make mental notes of good and bad approaches to teaching—especially in the sciences.

Since I will be teaching biology, I want my students to be excited about everything we know about life sciences, but I want them also to be excited about how much we don't know. From there, I want them to understand the reality and application of current biological research.

Katie was awarded her Master's in Teaching (MIT) from the University of Southern California on May 11, 2007, and signed on to teach science to students at-risk for the Los Angeles Unified School District.

Well, you did it. If you're reading this, you've completed all four parts of this life-changing program on how to be your own amazing mentor. Congratulations!

What you've learned in this book will provide you with the tools necessary for making significant changes and decisions in your life, provided you will:

Free Yourself!
Think for Yourself!
Reinvent Yourself!
And Ignite Yourself!

By completing these four parts of the program, you have become the lightning in the bottle I described in the Preface.

An Unothodox Guide to Becoming Your Own Mentor

I wrote this book because I believe that at some point men and women have to stop looking for advice outside of themselves. Life coaching advice is often overrated. Before you can learn what others know about what you think you don't know, you need to learn what you do know. Does that make sense? I wrote this book so that you could get the most out of your own inner-guidance system and dormant wisdom. As I look back on my life, I see that a good deal of what I have found most worthwhile, I figured out somehow for myself. For example, I learned grammar teaching grammar to business-writing students, and I coached many future authors well before I wrote my first book. The point is, if you find someone you can coach along on what it is you'd like to learn, you will learn faster what it is you want to learn, and it will be indelible in your mind.

Jackie Kennedy Onassis Mentored Herself

One of my heroes, Jackie Kennedy Onassis, never had a mentor in her lifetime. She was her own mentor. She insisted on engaging the best life coach available—the world itself. Jackie was a voracious reader and even in her thirties she became the primary creator of the world's most powerful political myth, called Camelot. She triumphed based on what she always taught herself, not on what Washington's politicians or the Kennedy family's rules might have placed upon her.

Being your own self mentor means *knowing when to hold 'em and knowing when to fold 'em,* as country singer Kenny Rogers sings it. All coaching and mentoring comes to an end. Someone stops giving, or someone outgrows the process. It's at that time you must be ready to become your own mentor.

The Perfect Companion Book to This One—
Discover True North

A few years ago, I wrote another book for McGraw-Hill, called *Discover True North: A 4-Week Approach to Ignite Your Passion and Activate Your Potential.* It is a powerful formula for successful living and career building, and I believe it is the perfect companion book to this one you have just read.

If you want to double your learning power, I highly recommend that after reading this book and completing the program you read *Discover True North* and begin that program as well. You will quickly find that the two programs are like building blocks that support one another's lessons. Reading both books and completing both programs will give you the depth and the breadth to kick everything up a level—career planning, self-mentoring, life coaching, and personal happiness.

Index